How to Start a Conversation and Make Friends

Don Gabor

illustrated by
Mary Power

A FIRESIDE BOOK
Published by Simon & Schuster
New York London Toronto Sydney Tokyo Singapore

FIRESIDE and colophon are registered trademarks of
Simon & Schuster, Inc.

Designed by *JUDY ALLAN (THE DESIGNING WOMAN)*

Manufactured in the United States of America

Printed and bound by Semline, Inc.

       17   19   20   18   16

Library of Congress Cataloging in Publication Data

Gabor, Don.
  How to start a conversation and make friends.
  "A Fireside book."
  1. Conversation. 2. Friendship. I. Title.
BJ2121.G3 1983 248.2'4   83-12038
ISBN: 0-671-47421-9

This book is dedicated to my family, friends, and my dog, Farina, for their stimulating conversations and support.

Acknowledgment

Special thanks to Jeffrey Hollander and "Network for Learning" for the opportunity to develop my conversation course and this book.

Contents

Introduction: Turn On and Tune In

THE NEXT TIME YOU WALK INTO A ROOM FULL OF PEOPLE, JUST listen to them talking! They're all communicating through conversation. Conversation is our main way of expressing our ideas, opinions, goals, and feelings to those we come into contact with. It is also the primary means of beginning and establishing friendships and relationships.

When the "channel of conversation" is open, we can connect and communicate with people around us. If the conversational channel is closed, then starting and sustaining a conversation can be a real problem. This book is based on my class, "How to Start a Conversation and Make Friends," and it will show you how to "turn on" your conversational channel and "tune in" to people you meet.

The conversational techniques in this book have been

successfully tested in my classes and proven as methods of starting and sustaining conversations in nearly every situation—including social and business settings. The techniques are presented in an easy-to-master format so you can start improving your communication skills and self-confidence quickly. The techniques are demonstrated in real-life situations so you can practice and learn them within the context of your own lifestyle and at your own pace.

This book can be helpful to a wide variety of people including

singles	managers
couples	students
professionals	parents
sales representatives	immigrants
consultants	freelance artists
teachers	business executives
	and many others.

Who attends my classes? Although many of the students may be "shy," most are people who want to improve their ability to communicate.

How This Book Can Help You

Many students who attend my classes are making career changes, and they want to learn how to move easily into a new social and work environment. Sales people want to know how to converse with clients in an informal (soft-sell) manner, while women executives want to feel confident communicating with their male associates on an equal and nonsexual basis. New residents of the United States want to learn conversational English. Business executives want to learn how not to talk shop while entertaining, and parents want to learn to communicate well with their children and other family members. The list seems endless.

If you can converse in most situations without much problem, you can further your business and personal goals by improving your conversational skills. Even good conversationalists sometimes find themselves in situations where the conversation is just not going the way they want it to. This book provides techniques to help you better direct and control the conversation at such times.

Learn to Enjoy Parties While Winning New Friends

Perhaps the most common situation that causes problems for many is meeting new people and socializing at cocktail parties and social events. Many people feel uncomfortable in a room full of strangers and are anxious about approaching others. This book discusses not just meeting new people, but making new friends, and developing lasting and meaningful relationships.

Most people want to share their experiences with others. We are constantly searching for others we can relate to on an intellectual, physical, and emotional level. This search can be frustrating and unfulfilling if you aren't able to reach out and communicate. Once you master the basic fundamentals of good conversation and are willing to reach out, you'll be open and available for new friendships and relationships.

You Can Learn to Communicate and Use New Skills

The ability to communicate in an informal and friendly manner is essential for every aspect of a person's business, social, and personal life. Most people can converse with others when they feel confident and comfortable. The problem arises when comfort and confidence are replaced by anxiety and fear. This book will help you identify which communication skills you already have working for you and in which situations you already feel confident.

Once you understand the skills that promote natural conversations, then begin using them in situations where you feel comfortable and confident. You will be able to see how effective you are, while simultaneously integrating these new techniques into your lifestyle.

As you become more confident with your conversational skills in "safe" situations, take some extra risks, and begin to use your new communication skills in situations where you were previously uncomfortable and anxious. You'll be pleasantly surprised to find that your skills will transfer from one situation to another without difficulty. As your control increases, so will your confidence. Your ability to maintain casual and sustained conversations will become part of your personality. Don't think about the skills and techniques; just let them become a subconscious basis for communicating.

Connect with People

The goal of conversation is to connect with people and the world around us. We have much to gain by communicating in an open and mutual manner. By sharing our experiences, we can grow in new ways. Our horizons and opportunities can expand, while our relationships may deepen and become more meaningful. Friendships and a sense of personal fulfillment can develop.

Conversation is also a means of negotiating with others. Communicating our wants and needs effectively is essential to fulfilling them.

Getting Started

Begin by opening your mind and your senses to people and the world around you. Begin to integrate your new skills into your personality. You don't have to become a different person. You just need to change your attitudes and skills when you deal with others. Be patient and focus on small daily changes, rather than waiting for revelations. Remember, our patterns have had many years to crystallize, and it takes time for them to change.

You must have the desire to change, reach out to others, and try some new ideas. Set a goal to make contact with others. With a background of basic communication skills, you will find that *accomplishing your goal is easier and more fun than you thought!* Let's begin and . . . start a conversation!

Closed body language sends out the message: "Stay away! I'd rather be left alone!"

1 Be Receptive— Body Language

O NE OF OUR MOST IMPORTANT CONVERSATIONAL SKILLS doesn't come from our tongue, but from our body. Research has shown that over 70 percent of communication is nonverbal. "Body language," as it is called, often communicates our feelings and attitudes before we speak, and it projects our level of receptivity to others.

Most poor conversationalists don't realize that their nonreceptive body language (closed posture, little eye contact, and no smiling) is often the cause of short and unsustained conversations. We are judged quickly by the first signals we give off, and if the first impressions are not positive and friendly, it's going to be difficult to maintain a good conversation. The following "softening" techniques can make your first impressions work *for* you, not against you.

S-O-F-T-E-N

A "softener" is a nonverbal gesture that will make people more responsive and receptive to you. Since your body language speaks before you do, it is important to project a positive and friendly image. When you use positive body language, you are already sending the signal: "I'm friendly and willing to communicate, if you are." Each letter in S-O-F-T-E-N represents a specific nonverbal technique for encouraging others to talk with you.

Research has shown that over 70 percent of communication is nonverbal.

S = Smile

A pleasant *smile* is a strong indication of a friendly and open attitude and a willingness to communicate. It is a positive, nonverbal signal sent with the hope that the other person will smile back. When you smile, you demonstrate

A smile shows you are friendly and open to communication. When you frown or wrinkle your brow, you give off signals of skepticism and nonreceptivity.

that you have noticed the person in a positive manner. The other person considers it a compliment and will usually feel good. The result? The other person will usually smile back.

Smiling does not mean that you have to put on a phony face or pretend that you are happy all of the time. But when you see someone you know, or would like to make contact with, do smile. By smiling, you are demonstrating an open attitude to conversation.

The human face sends out an enormous number of verbal and nonverbal signals. If you send out friendly messages, you're going to get friendly messages back. When you couple a warm smile with a friendly hello, you'll be pleasantly surprised by positive responses. It's the easiest way to show someone that you've noticed him in a positive way. A smile indicates a general approval toward the other person, and this will usually make the other person feel more receptive and friendly toward you.

O = Open Posture

The letter *O* in S-O-F-T-E-N stands for *open posture.* You might not realize that closed posture is the cause of many conversational problems. Typical closed posture is sitting with your arms and legs crossed, and your hand covering your mouth or chin. This is often called the "thinking pose," but just ask yourself this question: Are you going to interrupt someone who appears to be deep in thought? Not only does this posture give off "stay away" signals to others, but it also prevents your main "signal sender" (your mouth) from being seen by others looking for receptive conversa-

Closed posture: "I'm thinking and don't want to be disturbed. Stay away!"

Open posture: "I'm receptive and available for contact."

tional signals. Without these receptive signals, another person will most likely avoid you and look for someone who appears to be more available for contact. Closed posture discourages others from talking with you, and from approaching you in the first place. Closed posture can spell D-O-O-M for a conversation already in progress.

To overcome this habitual way of standing or sitting, start by keeping your hands away from your mouth, and keep your arms uncrossed. Crossed arms tend to indicate a defensive frame of mind, and thus one not particularly favorable to outside contact. They can also indicate impatience, displeasure, or judgment—any of which would discourage people from opening up.

Open posture is most effective when you place yourself within communicating distance of the other person—that is, within about five feet. Take care, however, not to violate someone's "personal space" by getting too close, too soon. Of course, if the situation calls for it, the closer, the better! However, be sensitive to the other person's body language, and the verbal and nonverbal signals she sends you. And remember too, there are cultural differences as to defining a comfortable distance for talking between strangers.

Some people will argue that just because they have "closed posture" doesn't mean they're defensive, uptight, or unreceptive to outside contact. They might say: "I stand this way because I am comfortable!" Whether you are really receptive or not, others can only interpret what they see. That's why people with closed posture tend to be seen as unreceptive to conversation. Open posture sends out the clear signals of openness and receptivity. It says: "I'm available for contact—come over and talk to me!"

F = Forward Lean

The letter *F* in S-O-F-T-E-N means *forward lean*, another element of open posture. Leaning forward slightly while a person is talking to you indicates interest on your part, and shows you are listening to what the person is saying. This is usually taken as a compliment by the other person, and will encourage him to continue talking.

Leaning back gives off signals of disinterest and even boredom.

Leaning forward says, "I'm interested in what you're saying."

Often people will lean back with their hands over their mouth, chin, or behind their head in the "thinking" pose. This posture gives off signals of judgment, skepticism, and boredom from the listener. Since most people do not feel comfortable when they think they are being judged, this leaning-back posture tends to inhibit the speaker from continuing.

It's far better to lean forward slightly in a casual and natural way. By doing this, you are saying: "I hear what you're saying, and I'm interested—keep talking!" This usually lets the other person feel that what he is saying is interesting, and encourages him to continue speaking.

T = Touch

The letter T in S-O-F-T-E-N stands for *touch*. In our culture, the most acceptable form of first contact between two people who are just meeting is a warm handshake. This is true when meeting members of the same or opposite sex—and not just in business, but in social situations, too. In nearly every situation, a warm and firm handshake is a safe and positive way of showing an open and friendly attitude toward the people you meet.

Be the first to extend your hand in greeting. Couple this with a friendly "Hi," a nice smile, and your name, and you have made the first step to open the channels of communication between you and the other person.

A friendly handshake coupled with a smile and a warm "Hello. . . . Nice to meet you" is an easy, acceptable form of touch when meeting someone for the first time.

Some men don't feel right in offering their hand to a woman first. They would feel stupid if the woman didn't shake their hand. Emily Post states in the revised edition of her book of etiquette that it is perfectly acceptable for a man to offer a handshake to a woman, and that it would be quite rude for either man or woman to ignore or refuse this friendly gesture.

Some women, on the other hand, feel that they are being

too forward if they offer a handshake to a man. They think the man might get the "wrong idea" if they extend their hand first in greeting. The problem is that there are two people who are afraid to shake hands. Of all the people I've polled on the subject in my class, there is nearly unanimous agreement: no matter who makes the first move, nearly everyone likes this form of physical contact. It's safe and nonthreatening for both parties. This keeps personal defenses down and creates an atmosphere of equality and receptivity between the people. More personal forms of touch should be exercised with sensitivity to the other person's body language, and in a warm, nonaggressive manner.

It is also important to end your conversations with a warm and friendly handshake, in business as well as social situations. Couple it with a bright smile and a friendly statement like, "I've really enjoyed talking with you!" or "Let's get together again soon!" This is an excellent way to end a conversation. You and the other person both feel good about the exchange.

E = Eye Contact

The letter E in S-O-F-T-E-N represents *eye contact*. The strongest of the nonverbal gestures are sent through the eyes. Direct eye contact indicates that you are listening to the other person, and that you want to know about her. Couple eye contact with a friendly smile, and you'll send this unmistakable message: "I'd like to talk to you, and maybe get to know you better."

Eye contact should be natural and not forced or overdone. It is perfectly okay to have brief periods of eye contact while you observe other parts of the person's face—particularly the mouth. When the person smiles, be sure to smile back. But always make an effort to return your gaze to the person's eyes as she speaks. It is common to look up, down, and all around when speaking to others, and it's acceptable not to have eye contact at all times.

Too much eye contact, especially if it is forced, can be

Eye contact shows that you are listening and taking an interest in what is being said. It sends the signal: "I'm listening—keep talking!"

counterproductive. If you stare at a person, or leer in a suspicious manner, the other person may feel uncomfortable and even suspicious about your intentions. A fixed stare can appear as aggressive behavior if it takes the form of a challenge as to who will look away first. It is not wise to employ eye contact as a "power trip," and will usually result in a negative, defensive response from the other person.

If you have a problem maintaining normal eye contact, try these suggestions. Start with short periods of eye contact—maybe only a few seconds. Look into the pupils of the other person's eyes, and smile. Then let your gaze travel over the features of her face, hair, nose, lips, and even earlobes! There is a six-inch diameter around the eyes that can provide a visual pathway. Remember, after a few moments, go back to looking the person right in the eyes. You can look back and forth between both eyes while increasing the amount of time that you experience direct eye contact as the conversation continues.

Avoiding eye contact can make both parties feel anxious and uncomfortable, and can give the impression that you are uninterested, dishonest, or bored with the conversation and the company. The result will usually be a short and unfulfilling conversation. So be sure to look into the eyes of the people you talk with, and send this message: "I hear what you're saying—go on!"

N = Nod

The letter N in S-O-F-T-E-N stands for *nod*. A nod of the head indicates that you are listening and that you understand what is being said. It signals approval and encourages the other person to continue talking. A nod of the head, coupled with a smile and a friendly hello, is an excellent way of greeting people on the street, or anywhere else. Like all the other softening gestures, it sends the same message: "I'm friendly and willing to communicate."

A nod of the head shows you are listening and understand what is being said. It sends the message: "I hear you, go on!"

Caution

Remember that these nonverbal softening gestures alone do not replace verbal communication. Moreover, if you only see isolated gestures, rather than clusters of gestures, your perception of receptivity may be incorrect. However, when you look for and use clusters of these softening gestures together with good conversational techniques, you will create an impression of openness and availability for contact and conversation.

With practice and a greater awareness of body language, you will be able to send and receive receptive signals, and encourage others to approach you and feel comfortable. Begin to notice other people's body language as well as your own. This will help you to identify softening techniques and recognize levels of receptivity in others, thus minimizing the chance of being rejected. Look for people who display receptive body language and project receptive body language by using softening techniques—they really work!!

Dear Gabby,

I'm at a cocktail party, and I don't know anyone. It seems like everybody knows everybody else, except me. How do I go up to someone and start a conversation?

Thank you,
Shy

Starting conversations at a party is easy if you remember to look for receptive faces among the crowd. Use plenty of eye contact, smile, and above all, keep your arms uncrossed and your hands away from your face. Begin to circulate around the room, checking out the people as you travel to the food table, bar, or dance area. Keep your eyes open for familiar and friendly faces. When you spot someone who looks open to contact (you are reading body language and looking for open posture), then casually stroll over to the person and say, "Hi, how you doin'?" or "Hello, how are you?" You can introduce yourself right then and there if you wish, or make a comment about the food, music, environment, or anything else you can focus on in the situation. You can also give the person a sincere compliment, and then follow it with a ritual question based on the situation. It might go something like this: "I couldn't help noticing what an attractive outfit you have on. I just wanted to come over and tell you how nice I think you look. Are you with one of the companies or here as an independent representative?"

2 Starting Conversations Naturally

S O NOW THAT YOU'RE TUNED IN TO THE CONVERSATIONAL channel of body language, how do you actually start a conversation? How do you break the ice?

There are five basic steps in starting conversations, which don't always occur in this order. *Establish eye contact and smile,* then follow this simple procedure.

1. *Risk versus rejection.* Be the first to say hello.
2. *Ritual questions.* Ask easy-to-answer questions about the situation, the other person, or yourself.
3. *Active listening.* Know what to say next by listening carefully for free information.
4. *Seek information.* Ask information-seeking follow-up questions based on free information *you've just heard.*
5. *Self-disclosure.* Reveal plenty of your free information while asking questions that may interest you personally.

An unenthusiastic response, or no reaction, is sure to kill a conversation.

1. Risk Versus Rejection

It takes a certain amount of risk to begin a conversation with a stranger. Most shy people don't start conversations because of the fear of being rejected. Of course, this prevents them from reaching out to others. Remember that risk taking and rejection are part of life, and to be overly sensitive is counterproductive. And, anyway, what's so bad about being rejected by someone you don't even know?

Change from Passive to Active

Most shy people take the passive role when it comes to starting conversations. They wait and wait and wait, hoping someone will come along and start a conversation with them. If there are two shy people together, they're both waiting, both taking the passive role. If someone else by chance does start talking, the shy person is often so surprised, she doesn't know what to say.

To get out of this "Catch-22," simply change from the passive to the active role. Be the first to say hello and take the initiative to begin the conversation. Introduce yourself to people regularly and begin to share your ideas, feelings, opinions, and experiences. Look for familiar faces, and after saying hello, seek out other people's thoughts, views, interests, and knowledge. By initiating conversations, you'll get more positive responses, and your fear of rejection will lessen. In this way your risk taking can pay off in making new contacts and having more meaningful conversations.

Another advantage of being the first to say hello is that it gives you the opportunity to guide the direction of the conversation, and gives the other person the impression that you are friendly and open. You are also complimenting the other person by showing interest in a positive way.

Minimize Rejections—
Look for Receptivity

The more you start conversations, the more positive responses you will get. But, of course, there are going to be some rejections too. No one receives unanimous approval, so when you do get rejected, don't dwell on it. Instead, use it as a lesson and plan a different approach next time.

The most important way to minimize rejection is to look for receptivity in those you approach. Try to be sensitive to "where others are at." Look for an open posture, eye contact, and a smile. Look for people who are sending receptive signals through their body language, and when you feel the time is right, approach them in a friendly and direct way. For example, if you are at a party or dance, and would like to ask someone for a dance, then look to those who either are dancing or look like they want to dance. Wait for the moment when the person seems most receptive, and then take the risk. Move closer to the person and establish eye contact, smile, and ask the person for a dance. Chances are the other person may feel flattered that you have noticed him, and hopefully will respond positively. If, however, the answer is no, then accept it gracefully with a smile (like water off a duck's back), and ask someone else. Keep asking and you're bound to get a positive response. The more you ask, the better you'll get at picking out people who will respond positively to you.

How to Accept Rejections

If you have been rejected many times in your life, then one more rejection isn't going to make much difference. If you're rejected, don't automatically assume it's your fault. The other person may have several reasons for not doing what you are asking him to do; none of it may have anything to do with you. Perhaps the person is busy or not feeling well or genuinely not interested in spending time with you. Rejections are part of everyday life. Don't let them bother you. Keep reaching out to others. When you begin to receive positive responses, then you are on the right track. It's all a matter of numbers. Count the positive responses and forget about the rejections.

This simple philosophy can help people who fear rejection. If you have only taken a few social risks and have been rejected once or twice, then those rejections loom very large in your life. If, on the other hand, you take more risks, and start conversations, you will receive a mixture of positive and negative responses, and each rejection will become less and less meaningful. Focus on the positive responses, and you will get better at choosing receptive people.

You really have very little to lose and a lot to gain.

Taking the risk to be the first to say hello isn't such a fearful step. When you take the active role, you are sending this message: "I'm friendly and willing to communicate if you are."

2. Ask Easy-to-Answer Ritual Questions

Ritual questions are easy-to-answer requests for information. Although basically requests for personal background or general information, their real purpose is to convey this message: "I'm interested in getting to know you better."

Breaking the Ice—A Compliment Followed by a Ritual Question

Ritual questions can be used to break the ice with someone you don't know and wish to speak to. The easiest way to start a conversation with a stranger is to employ one of the three following ways. First, notice something positive about the person you wish to speak with, and in a friendly and sincere manner, offer a compliment about what she is doing, wearing, or saying. Quickly follow the compliment with a ritual question that is directly related to the compliment you just gave. The "opening line" might be: "That's a beautiful ring you're wearing! What kind of stone is it?" or "Say, you're a terrific skater! How did you learn to do all those tricks?"

A second way to break the ice is to notice something that the person is carrying—maybe a book, musical instrument, or a piece of sporting equipment. After establishing eye contact and smiling, ask a ritual question based on the object. For example, if you see someone with a tennis racket, you could say something like: "Say, could you recommend a good place to take tennis lessons?" or "Do you know a good place to play without having to wait for a court?" or "I notice

A compliment followed by an easy-to-answer ritual question is a good way to break the ice.

you have a racket like the one I'm interested in buying. How do you like it?" or "I see you're a tennis player. I want to start playing. Can you recommend a good racket for a beginner?"

If you see someone carrying a book, you can ask how he likes it. If a person has a musical instrument, you can ask him what kind of music he plays, where he plays or studies, how long he has been playing, or how you might get involved. If you see someone with a camera, you could ask him if he has taken any good pictures, about the type of camera he has, or if he is a professional or amateur photographer. These questions can be applied to almost any object a person is carrying. It is a safe and positive way of showing someone you've noticed him, while breaking the ice and starting a conversation at the same time.

A third way to break the ice and start a conversation is to make a comment, or ask a question based on the situation. This can be a request for information like: "Say, excuse me, but I'm looking for an apartment in the neighborhood. Do you happen to know of any places that might be for rent?" Or another common question might be: "I'm looking for a good place to eat nearby. Can you recommend a restaurant in the neighborhood?" If you see someone who looks like she needs some assistance, then offering help is an excellent way to start a conversation. You might say: "You look a little lost. Are you looking for someplace in particular? I live in the neighborhood—maybe I can help you."

Dear Gabby,

I'm dining alone at a restaurant. I see someone who appears to be alone, too. How do I ask if she wants to join me for dinner?

Sincerely yours,
Lonely

When you enter a restaurant and you're alone, look around for another solo diner reading the menu, having a drink, reading the paper, or just gazing off into space. Make an effort to be seated near the person, and when she looks in your direction, make eye contact and smile. If the response seems positive, you can lean over (if you are close enough) and say, "This is my first time here. Can you recommend something good?" Or if it is a foreign restaurant you can ask, "Excuse me, but I don't read French. Would you help me translate?" If the person seems open to you, then ask, "Are you waiting for someone?" and if she answers no, then say, "Would you care to join me? I have a good bottle of wine that I'd be happy to share."

Many people dine alone frequently. If you approach someone in a friendly and low-pressured way, she may be quite open to your invitation. Offer to buy the person a drink to show her that you are really interested in having her join you. It is only a friendly gesture and doesn't necessarily mean that you are treating her to dinner.

In addition to asking for or offering assistance, you can

make comments based on what you observe. It is best to focus on the positive things you see rather than complaining about the negative. This way you can let others in on the way you see the world, and not get caught in a conversation of "Ain't it a shame!" If you happen to be standing in a movie line, you can comment on other films, or the most recent book you've read if you are browsing in a bookstore. Another comment you can make that is very direct is: "I've seen you here before. Do you live or work around here?"

Ritual questions are good for breaking the ice and starting a conversation. By looking for what people are involved in, you can easily focus on a topic of interest to the other person. Remember, in addition to finding out about the other person, you are sending this signal: "You seem interesting to me, and I'd like to get to know you better!"

Closed and Open Ritual Questions

You might find yourself asking ritual question after ritual question, and only getting one- or two-word answers. This is probably because you are asking "closed-ended" ritual questions instead of "open-ended" ritual questions.

Closed-ended ritual questions usually require only a yes or a no, or just a one- or two-word answer. These are useful for breaking the ice, but they should be followed with an open-ended question. *Open-ended* ritual questions usually require more than a brief answer, and they encourage the other person to elaborate on his answer. In addition, they provide an opportunity to reveal facts, opinions, feelings, and most important, plenty of free information. Closed-ended questions often begin with words like: Are? Do? Who? Where? and Which? Open-ended ritual questions commonly start with How? Why? In what way? How did you get involved? How can I get involved? "What" can be used as both an open and closed-ended question.

Here are some common examples of closed-ended ritual questions.

DO YOU LIVE AROUND HERE?
DO YOU LIKE THE FOOD?
WHAT TIME IS IT?
ARE YOU GOING TO THE PARK?
WHEN DID YOU GET HERE?
WHERE ARE YOU FROM?
ARE YOU ENJOYING YOUR STAY HERE?

Here are some examples of *open-ended* ritual questions.

HOW DID YOU FIND YOUR APARTMENT?
IN WHAT WAYS DO YOU THINK THIS COUNTRY HAS CHANGED?
HOW DID YOU GET INVOLVED IN THAT LINE OF WORK?
WHY DID YOU DECIDE TO MOVE THERE?
WHAT BRINGS YOU TO NEW YORK?
WHAT DO YOU LIKE TO DO ON YOUR DAYS OFF?

These are just a few examples of closed- and open-ended ritual questions. Remember to follow closed questions with open-ended questions. In this way you can fish for topics of interest and then seek further information by asking open-ended questions.

It is very important to be able to answer ritual questions, too. Make your questions easy and straightforward. Most people are far more comfortable answering expected, easy-to-answer questions when they first meet a person, rather than difficult or complicated questions that put them on the spot.

Some people think that they may offend the other person if they ask ritual questions. They say they don't want to be too personal or pry. In most cases, the opposite is true. Most people feel flattered when someone notices them in a positive way and shows a genuine interest. This usually encourages the person to talk.

Free Information

When we communicate with one another, we reveal much more than we realize. The information that we volunteer is called *free information*. When you ask or answer a ritual question, be aware of the free information that accompanies the answer. Focus on this, and use it as conversational fuel for follow-up questions. By focusing on the free information we can explore each other's experiences and interests in a natural and free-flowing manner.

Telling Others What You Do

Some people feel uncomfortable telling or asking others what they do, and some are offended when they are asked this common ritual question. This defensive and closed attitude is not conducive to opening the channels of conversation, and will ultimately be a barrier to communication.

Don't be uptight and resistant to this type of ritual question. It is better to tell others what you do in a few short sentences, revealing plenty of free information for the other person to pick up on. You can reveal basic facts about yourself, while guiding the direction of the conversation. If you insist on not disclosing this information, the other party will slowly become suspicious (especially if he has given out that information) or lose interest in trying to get to know you. If you expect to be friends with this person, how long can you withhold this basic information?

Many people who don't like to tell others what they do are also anxious about other types of ritual questions. They feel small talk is dull and boring, and should be avoided. Instead, they say they want to talk about something important.

While there isn't a particular order as to how conversations should proceed, most conversations that do not go through the "ritual" phases rarely proceed to deeper and more meaningful levels. Small talk is a very important element in conversations and in establishing friendships and relationships.

Getting to Know You

Ritual questions allow you to reveal basic personal information in a natural and informal way. By exchanging little details about one another, you can get to know the person you are talking with very quickly. Ritual questions help you quickly determine if you would like to get to know this person better. Ritual questions help you to find out and disclose personal backgrounds, and provide an opportunity to discover the "big things" in a person's life. Asking ritual questions is like fishing—you may have to cast a few times before you get a bite, but once you do, look out!

Ask ritual questions when you want to break the ice or change topics in conversation. If your ritual question gets a brief response, try another until you get an enthusiastic response. When you discover an area of interest in the other person, be sure to follow with an open-ended information-seeking question. When the topic seems to be running out of steam (you don't have to talk a topic completely out), return to another ritual question based on free information that you or the other person revealed earlier.

Ritual questioning prepares you to introduce yourself to the other person. Usually, the sooner the better. When there is a pause in the conversation, this is a good time to say: "By the way, my name is _____. What's yours?" The other person will almost certainly respond in kind. If your hand is free, offer a handshake, a friendly smile, and say: "Nice to meet you, _____!" Use the person's name right away, and as often as you can *without overdoing it.* This will help you to remember his name, and using a person's name is one of the easiest and most meaningful compliments you can give. If you do forget a person's name, it's perfectly okay to say: "Excuse me, but what's your name again?"

If you employ these ritual question techniques for breaking the ice with the people you meet, you'll discover they really do work. Being the first to say hello won't be a problem any longer.

3. Know What to Say by Listening (Active Listening)

Okay, so you ask a few ritual questions, then what do you say? You always seem to run out of things to talk about in less than a minute! You can never think of what to say next!

Don't Think—Listen!

Know what to say next by listening carefully for key words, facts, opinions, feelings, and most of all, free information. Don't think about what you are going to say next, because while you are thinking, you're not listening! Most shy people are usually so preoccupied with—"Oh no, it's going to be my turn to talk soon, and I won't know what to say!"— that they don't hear what the other person is saying.

The solution to this problem is to use *active listening skills* while the other person is speaking. These include using good body language, especially eye contact, smiling, and nodding in response. Active listening encourages people to continue speaking, and it shows that your attention is focused on the conversation. By asking quick information-seeking questions, you can keep the details of the conversation close at hand. When you understand the point the person is making, restate it in another way by saying: "Do you mean to say . . . ?" or "Now if I understand you correctly. . . ."

Improve Your Listening Skills

Conversation problems include poor listening, memory, and concentration skills. There is usually enough time for your mind to wander while you are being spoken to, and many people speak slowly and with lengthy pauses between thoughts. The result is that your mind may wander. You can lose your concentration and even the main idea of the conversation.

Don't Be a Parrot

Some people try to maintain their attention by repeating each word the other person says. This is parroting and is more a waste of mental energy than actually an aid to listening and concentration. You can remember details and concepts better if you listen for key words and main ideas.

Merge Old Knowledge with New Information

Your listening, concentration, and memory will improve considerably if your mind is active and alert, and if you are participating in the conversation. Be sure to interject your thoughts into the conversation, while linking the new information with previously known information. This synthesis of prior knowledge and new information will provide you with a framework for remembering the details you hear and a basis for asking follow-up questions.

Use Examples

Ask for and think of examples that support or question what is being said. If you are not sure what the other person is saying, or you don't understand what she is talking about, ask for an example to make the point clear for you.

Anticipate

A good listener is actively involved in the conversation, and can often anticipate what the speaker is going to say next. This involvement shows concern and interest, and will usually reinforce facts and details. Take care not to complete sentences for people you are talking with if they pause for a moment to construct their words. If you anticipated the speaker correctly, then you know you are probably on the same wave length. If your anticipations were not correct, this can be a warning signal that you and your partner are not tuned in to each other, and that a misunderstanding may be developing.

Summarize

It is not uncommon for people talking to wander off the main topic. When you are listening, it is helpful to keep the main theme in mind, and from time to time, summarize. You can say something like: "It sounds to me like you are . . . Am I right?" This focuses your listening skills, and helps you remember details and the main ideas of the conversation.

Get Actively Involved

By being aware and actively involved in a conversation, you bring your critical faculties into action. This requires you to connect what the speaker is saying with what you already know. Then take note of what you agree and/or disagree with. This is especially important when discussing current events and controversial topics.

Listen for "Iceberg" Statements

An "iceberg" statement is a comment or a piece of free information where 90 percent is under the surface, waiting to be asked about. Iceberg statements usually come in the form of one or two words that accompany answers to ritual questions. These statements are hints about topics that the person really wants to talk about if she thinks you might be interested. When you hear an iceberg statement like, "You'll never believe what happened to me . . ." or "Guess what I've been doing," quickly ask a related follow-up question or say: "What happened?" or "You don't say! Tell me, how was it?" Other "continuers" are: "Why do you say that?" "In what ways?" and "How so?"

Dear Gabby,

How do I enter a conversation at a cocktail party when two or three people are discussing current events?

Thank you,
Yearning to be Involved.

To enter a conversation in progress, you must be within listening and speaking range. Move close to the people speaking and show interest in what is being said. Use plenty of eye contact, nodding, and smiling to send the signal to the speaker that you want to hear more. Often, when a speaker sees you are interested in what he is saying, he will begin to include you as a listener.

When there is a pause, or the speaker says something you can respond to, then interject your comment or question into the conversation. If you use easy-to-answer information questions, the answers will be directed to you specifically. Say something like, "What did you do then?" or "How did you arrive at that conclusion?" or "That's a truly incredible story! How long ago did this happen?"

You may be saying to yourself that this is an intrusion into a private conversation. If you have listened and carefully observed the people, you will quickly be able to determine whether the situation is open or closed. In many cases, especially at parties, the speaker is searching for others to interact with, and a new person who shows interest in participating is usually welcome.

Caution: Be careful not to play devil's advocate—that is, to take an opposition position for the sake of argument. This usually leads to a tense and competitive conversation, with a winner and a loser. You won't be considered a welcome addition to a conversation with a group of strangers if you make them look stupid in front of their friends.

Good Listening Requires
Practice and Concentration

Active listening skills need to be practiced and will aid your conversational abilities immensely. They will encourage those you talk with to elaborate further and to feel more comfortable in opening up to you. When you share a person's enthusiasm for a topic by listening closely to what he says, you are giving him a "green light" to continue and really "get into it." Active listening shows your interest and

curiosity in a person by sending this message: "I'm interested in what you are saying—keep talking, I'm willing to
listen!"

4. Seek More Information Based on Free Information

After you have broken the ice, asked a few ritual questions, and used active listening, then seek further information based on the free information you have learned.
By taking advantage of free information, you can control
the direction of the conversation. Ask open-ended questions that refer to the free information either you or your
conversation partner has revealed.

Free information is communicated by a person's clothing, physical features, body language, personal behavior,
and activities, as well as by her words. Sometimes free information will consist of a general impression. Then you
can say something like: "You seem to know a lot about
_____. Are you involved with _____?"
or "You sound like an expert. Do you teach a class on that
subject?" or "Are you a professional?"

Always try to follow closed-ended ritual questions with an
open-ended ritual question, to give your partner a chance
to elaborate on the topic. Pay close attention to facts, details, and especially more free information, with the idea of
directing the conversation into areas of mutual interest.

When discussing areas of professional interest, take care
not to "pick the person's brain." Don't ask for free advice on
a particular problem you are having. For example, if you
meet a dentist, DON'T say: "Oh, you're a dentist! How con-
venient! Say, I've got this sore tooth here, and I was won-
dering, as long as we are here, would you take a look?" Most
professionals don't mind telling others what they do, and
even discussing their work if they think you are interested,
but they resent being hit up for a free office visit.

Asking Personal Questions

Asking personal questions always requires a particular sensitivity to the other person's feelings, and especially his level of receptivity to you. It is usually best to preface personal questions with a softener like, "Excuse me for asking, but . . ." or "I'd love to know, if you don't mind telling me . . . ?" or "I hope I'm not being too personal, but . . . ?" or "Please feel free not to answer, but . . . ?" or "If you don't mind my asking . . . ?"

If you ask a personal question in such a way that the other person does not have to answer, often he will respond in some form. It may not be the direct answer you are looking for, because many people have trouble saying what they really mean, especially if it's personal. However, if you listen carefully for free information and look for receptive body language, you can get an idea about whether the person is ready to reveal some personal information to you.

Dear Gabby,

How do you gracefully tell someone she is asking questions that are too personal?

Thank you,
Private Person

If you are asked a question you'd rather not answer, simply say, "I'd rather not answer that question, if you don't mind." Most people will accept this statement as a courteous way of saying, "Mind your own business." If you are asked how much something costs and you'd rather not discuss it, say "It was a gift" or "Too much" or "Not enough."

A word of caution: Many people are overly concerned about revealing certain ritual information such as their occupation, home, etc. Don't be defensive about answering these "signals of interest" questions.

If you feel a question is too personal to answer, or you'd

rather not, it is your right to do as you wish. After declining to answer, throw the conversational ball back to the other person with a ritual question on a new topic.

Disclose your hopes, dreams, loves, joys, and sorrows, and people will be able to identify with you. We all share these basic emotional experiences.

Avoid Pitfalls When Seeking Information

Avoid traditional conversational taboos such as death, gory crimes, unhappy events, personal gossip, or racial and ethnic slurs. Avoid getting things off your chest and "unloading." It is best not to overdramatize regular daily events in your life or call attention to problems that your conversational partner cannot easily solve. These interactions can create a negative impression on your partner. Remember that it's better to begin with easy questions that will allow your partner to feel comfortable and allow you both to get to know each other through gradual self-disclosure.

An excellent way to get to know the interests and topics a person may wish to avoid discussing is to ask information-seeking questions. Be sensitive to the other person's feelings, and don't make him just answer question after question. A "cross-examination" can turn the other person off and usually occurs when you ask too many closed-ended ritual questions.

5. Disclose Free Information

Self-disclosure completes the conversational cycle of taking risks, asking ritual questions, active listening, and seeking information.

It's a Way to Let Others Get to Know You

Self-disclosure lets others get to know you on your own terms. The information you share with the people you meet determines how they get to know you. Be positive (without boasting) when you share your personal interests and the "big" events in your life, including your hopes, goals, and most rewarding experiences. You can tell others what you do for employment, your background, goals, and most importantly, your availability for future contact.

To Tell or Not to Tell— That Is the Question

Some people have "habitual secrecy," maintaining a veil of secrecy so others don't glimpse their thoughts and feelings. Often, caution about revealing certain aspects of one's background is positive, since it's necessary to keep certain information private, for business and personal reasons. Exercise discretion about what you tell others. No one expects you to tell everything about yourself, but the secretive person may feel safer not telling anything to anybody.

You may believe that (1) if other people knew what you were really like, they would think less of you and perhaps actively dislike you; (2) being too familiar with another person breeds contempt, so it is best to remain mysterious; or (3) if others knew intimate and personal facts about you, they would use this information against you. These fears allow you to feel safer if you remain secretive, since to make self-disclosing statements would be dangerous.

Realistically, What Do You Have to Lose?

Think about how many secrets you really have. Suppose you reveal some aspect of your life that you hadn't intended to disclose to a friend or acquaintance. What's likely to happen? Could this person use this information against you, and if so, what would she do? People who have trouble disclosing personal information place much more importance on it than the details warrant. Once you take a look at what is being revealed, the details aren't secrets that must be kept. Close and meaningful relationships are nearly impossible without personal revelations and mutual trust and confidence. Trust is created by being willing to reveal personal information to the other person. While some feelings are best kept to oneself, especially in work-related situations, it can be destructive to let this guarded attitude carry over into your personal life. Although there are people who do take unfair advantage of others' personal disclosures, avoiding sharing personal feelings is a guarantee to a life of loneliness and detachment.

To overcome this problem, begin to observe others as they disclose information to you and others. See how often you bury your feelings and opinions. Take the risk of being more open with your disclosures. The next time someone asks you a question about your background, personal feelings, or opinions, remember you are entitled to think and feel as you please. You are free to express yourself to others.

Self-Disclosure—Four Levels

There are four levels of self-disclosure that we use daily. The first is called "cliché" greeting. These are very general disclosures and are responses to ritual greetings such as: "How are you?" "How are you doing?" "How have you been?" or "How's the family?" Though these questions evoke responses such as "Fine!" or "Just great, couldn't be better," they provide an excellent opportunity to reveal free information. These low-level disclosures tell the other person that your attitude is open and friendly, and if the situation permits, that you are available for conversation.

After people exchange greetings, they usually exchange basic personal facts. Tell others what you do, where you are from, what you like to do for fun, or some current project or activity that you are involved in. This second level of self-disclosure provides a background of experiences and information for conversational partners to compare and explore. It is at this point that people begin to get to know one another.

The third level of self-disclosure is revealing personal opinions and preferences on different subjects. At this level you can reveal your attitudes, values, and concerns. You can tell others what you honestly think and feel about the world around us. Express your ideas in an open manner and encourage others to share their ideas on varied topics. Remember, people have differing views. Good conversation is *not a debate,* with a winner and a loser, but an exchange of views and ideas. Open-minded discussion, not arguing, is an excellent means of sustaining a conversation, while letting the participants know more about one another on a more meaningful level.

The final level of self-disclosure is your personal feelings —especially about the people you know and wish to become closer to. These are the most difficult disclosures to make because they require revealing our emotions. Though it can be difficult (and risky) to reveal your feelings, it will give your partners a more meaningful sense of who you are, and what you are sensitive to. When you disclose your hopes, dreams, loves, joys, and sorrows, people will be able to identify with you, because we all share these basic emotional experiences. When you disclose your feelings, use the words "I" and "feel" to describe how you feel and think. Many people make the common mistake of using the word "you" when they mean "I." When this happens, the partner doesn't know whom you are talking about.

Helpful Self-Disclosure Hints

Be Careful About How Much You Disclose

Don't go to the opposite extreme of "telling all." We've all had the experience of someone telling us her life story—and we know how uncomfortable this can be. It's better to reveal your background and ideas a little at a time and within the context of the conversation.

Be Realistic About Yourself

If you exaggerate your good qualities and hide your faults people will soon realize that you are not being real. It's important to *be yourself.* Sometimes people won't believe what you tell them, so disclose specific details including names, dates, and places. Balance the picture of yourself that you present. Let the discussion continue along with your self-disclosures so that you're certain your partner is taking you seriously.

Reveal Your Goals

Reveal your goals and struggles. You'll be surprised to learn that most people empathize with you and will usually be encouraging. The person you are talking with may be able to assist you in some way. By the same token, you may be able to assist your partner with his goals. If you can help someone else, you're certain to make a friend right away!

Let Someone Get to Know You

Don't be afraid of boring the other person. Most people are interested in making new friends, and it's essential to let others know who you are and if you have mutual interests. *You don't have to entertain the people you meet*, but be as upbeat as possible. Most people value personal contact. When you share aspects of your life with another person, you are making this all-important contact with her.

The following sample dialogue identifies the four levels of self-disclosure.

(greeting)	**D:** Hi, Bill! How's it going?
(greeting)	**B:** Oh, okay, Don, how are you?
(greeting)	**D:** Pretty busy right now. I'm teaching my conversation class tonight. What are you up to these days?
(fact)	**B:** I'm looking for a job. I'm a teacher, too.
(fact)	**D:** Oh really! What do you teach?
(feeling)	**B:** I taught business math, but I'm
(preference)	through with that. I can't stand it any
(opinion)	more—it's so boring! And I can't take the public school system any more! It drives me crazy!

(opinion)   **D:** I know what you mean. I loved the kids, but I didn't like the "system" either. I think it holds a lot of kids back from doing their best.

(opinion)   **B:** Not just the kids! I think it held me back from doing my best, too! Except when I was coaching the tennis team. Tennis is my real love.

(preference)   **D:** So you're looking for a job teaching tennis?

(preference)   **B:** If I could find one, I'd be in heaven. It's what I really want to do, but I'm not sure how to go about finding the job. I know

(feeling)   I could teach a great class if someone would just give me the chance.

(opinion)   **D:** I bet an adult tennis class would be really popular. Why don't you call the "Network for Learning." They might be interested.

(opinion)   **B:** I might give that a try. People are more health-conscious than they used to be. I'm a pretty good player. Do you play tennis?

(preference)
(feeling)   **D:** I've played a little. I like it. I have fun and stay in shape at the same time. The only problem is I don't have a steady partner.

(preference)   **B:** Hey, why don't we get together and play? We could have a lot of fun. I could give you some tips.

(preference)   **D:** That sounds like a great idea! How about tomorrow morning?

(preference)   **B:** All right. I'll meet you at 11:00 right here. How's that?

(opinion)   **D:** Sounds good! And good luck with your job hunting. I'm sure you'll find something if you keep looking.

(feeling)   **B:** I'm going to call the "Network for Learn-

ing" right now. Thanks for the tip—I appreciate your help. See you tomorrow!

(feeling)   **D:** Okay! I'm looking forward to the game.

(closing)   **B:** See you later! I'm going to try to get that job!

3 Keeping the Conversation Going

ONCE YOU'VE BROKEN THE ICE BY SAYING HELLO AND MAKING a comment or asking a few questions, do you get "tongue tied"?

Sustaining conversations is easy if you know the key factors involved. Of course, good body language, displaying interest and curiosity, and being friendly and enthusiastic are essential. Here are six additional keys to sustaining conversations easily and naturally.

1. Focus on the situation you are in.
2. Find out about the "big" events in the other person's life.
3. Balance the two-way information exchange.
4. Discuss topics that are important to you.
5. Change topics using free information.
6. Seek out common interests and experiences.

Key No. 1: Focus on the Situation You Are In

Begin by identifying yourself in your immediate environment, that is, right in the room or place where you happen to be. Why are you here? What activities take place here? How did you come to be in this place? What makes this place unusual or interesting? What can you find out about this place from someone else? What previous experiences have you had in this place? How do you feel about this place?

You can converse with others simply by focusing on the various aspects of your immediate surroundings. Once you identify yourself, it's natural to find out what others are doing in this place. This approach can provide many conversational topics. You don't have to think of *what* to say. Just observe your situation and find something to ask or comment about.

Look Outward—Not Inward

Many poor conversationalists tend to look and think inward rather than focusing on surrounding people and events. They think about how they look, what others might think about them, and whether they are liked. They wonder if people will think they are intelligent or stupid, attractive or ugly, and so on. These "self-centered" thoughts will make you feel self-conscious and almost totally unaware of what is occurring around you. As a result, all that conversational fuel right in front of your eyes, ears, and nose is lost. Once you begin to look outward with your senses, you become aware of the vast details that can become elements of conversation. In addition, when you think and look outward, you'll be less self-conscious and uncomfortable. Your self-confidence will increase, fear and self-doubt will diminish, and your conversations will become more natural and sustained.

Your Situation Is Really a Series of Concentric Circles

If you focus your conversation on your immediate surroundings, it's easy to expand your topics to the next immediate environment. For example, if you're in an adult education class, then the classroom is your immediate environment. After you discuss the class, broaden the conversation to include the school or neighborhood. Focus on the various elements of your surroundings—other classes, the campus, restaurants in the area, movie theaters, clubs, etc. As you continue, broaden your discussion to include where you live, how you travel to class, recreational areas nearby, the city, or interesting outlying areas. Once you realize the enormous amount of conversational fuel directly available, you'll never be at a loss for words.

For example, suppose this is your first time at the health club, and you've finally signed up for that exercise class you've been promising yourself for months. An attractive member of the opposite sex is next to you in line. Finding out what the other person hopes to gain from the class is a good beginning. After making eye contact and smiling, say hello and ask a question or make a comment based on your immediate situation. Be sure to volunteer your own goals too. The conversation might go something like this:

Don: Hi! Are you signing up for the beginning racketball class?

Mary: I sure am! I've been waiting to learn how to play this game right for a long time—and now I'm finally going to do it. What about you?

Don: Me, too! I've always been curious about this health club. I drive by it every day on my way to work, so I thought I'd give it a try. Have you taken classes here before?

Mary: I took a swimming course here last summer, and I really enjoyed it. The instructors were excellent, and I met a lot of nice people—plus I learned how to swim!

Don: I'm glad you're giving the place a good report. I'm looking forward to this racketball class. By the way, my name's Don.

Mary: How do you do. I'm Mary. Have you played racketball before?

Don: Not really. I've played a bit of tennis, and a little squash. I like racket games, so I figured it would be fun to learn racketball. Besides, I want to find a regular playing partner, and I thought that this would be a good way to find one. What brings you to the racketball class?

Mary: A friend told me it's pretty easy to learn and great exercise. Plus I really want to meet new people, so here I am! I think the class is going to be a lot of fun.

Don: I'm curious, Mary. Do you know if the food in the club lounge is any good? I'm always starved after a good workout.

Mary: I've heard it's pretty good, but I've never tried it.

Don: Well, if you're interested, maybe we could meet for a bite to eat or a cold drink after class? The treat's on me!

Mary: Sure! That sounds like a great idea! I'll meet you in front of the lounge.

Don: All right! See you after class!

In Don's conversation with Mary, they discussed reasons for taking the class, previous experience with racket games, the staff at the club, the food in the lounge, and finally a planned meeting for later. Based on the free information disclosed during the conversation, here are some more questions or comments that could have sustained the conversation for a much longer period of time:

What do you think of the club facilities?
Have you been taking classes here for a long time?
What other activities do they have here?
Do you live in the area?
Where do you work?

Do you know where there are some good restaurants in the area?

Do you have other racketball partners?

What kind of work do you do?

What do you do on your days off?

Would you like to meet for a game sometime?

Can I give you a ride home?

Key No. 2: Find Out About the Big Events in the Person's Life

Hot Buttons

Dale Carnegie in *How To Win Friends and Influence People* said if you find the really big events in a person's life, conversation won't be a problem. "Hot buttons" are areas which are of keen interest to and create enthusiasm in people you talk with and in yourself. These are subjects that you or your conversational partner can really "get into" and talk about for an extended period of time. Hot buttons can be work, a new job, a hobby, a career goal, an upcoming trip, a sporting activity, a personal dedication to a social cause, and even sex! Hot buttons are subjects or activities that really interest people. A hot button can be a lifelong interest, a passing fancy, or a current fascination—whatever turns you on! What do you like to do for fun or profit?

It's important to find other people's hot buttons as soon as possible because these strong interests are extremely fertile areas for sustained conversations. The sooner you find the other person's hot buttons and reveal your own, the more energetic and stimulating conversations you'll have—and you might discover that you share some strong personal interests.

One goal of asking ritual questions is to discover the other person's hot buttons. When you know someone's hot button, you know how to "turn him on" and you also find out what he considers important. You discover where he puts his time, money, and effort—that is, what he values. This is bountiful fuel for conversation, and it tells you about the person you're speaking with.

In addition to finding out what turns a person on, search for common goals, experiences, and ideas. People often have many topics they're interested in and willing to talk about. Since we all share common interests, it's important to fish for hot buttons in others. When you find someone with hot buttons similar to yours, you'll be able to find out if he would like to share those activities and interests with you. This is where friendships begin to develop.

How to Find
Someone Else's Hot Buttons

When you walk into a room full of strangers, do you say to yourself: "I don't have anything in common with the people here!"? Many people think their interests are unique and that others could care less. The opposite is usually true. Because of our accessibility to many different activities and interests, many people share common interests, goals, and life experiences. The trick is to find out about others, and discover which ones you have in common.

When seeking someone's hot buttons, fish around subject areas with ritual questions. When you receive a response that indicates your partner can "get into it," express interest in the subject. This doesn't mean you must have a strong interest in that subject, but it helps if you can generate a medium or slight curiosity in the subject. This allows the other person an opportunity to share some important aspects of her life with you, and will create positive feelings towards you. Your partner will feel that you care about her, and hopefully, she will express a similar interest in you.

Often people wear or carry items that are hot button indicators. Look for buttons, tennis rackets, books, jewelry, clothing, or anything that might provide a clue to the person's hot button. People participate in activities that are hot buttons. Focus on these activities by asking open-ended ritual questions, and sustaining conversations will be easy. Look for people having fun and striving for self-improvement or personal gain, and you'll be closer to finding a person's hot button.

Often people reveal their hot buttons through iceberg statements—that is, they make a statement that reveals the tip of the conversational iceberg, and they're just waiting to be asked the particulars of an activity or project they are involved in. Listen carefully for free information and ask open-ended follow-up questions to encourage people to talk about what they're into. You can say: "That's something I've always been curious about. How did you get involved?"

If there are few visual or verbal clues to a person's hot buttons, I suggest fishing with ritual questions and then asking something like: "What do you like to do on your days off?" or "What do you like to do for fun?" or "What do you like to do when you're not working?" These comments signal the other person that you're willing to listen and are interested in finding out more about what's important to them.

How You Can Reveal
Your Hot Buttons to Others

It's not enough to find the other person's hot buttons. Remember, a good conversation is balanced, so be ready to reveal your hot buttons, too. By letting others know what's important to you, you are giving them an opportunity to get to know you *on your terms* and in a way that is usually considered positive.

When you are invited to a party or social event, it can be helpful to think about what you're excited about and be willing to share this excitement with those you meet. Take a personal inventory of your hot buttons—projects, future plans, or world events—and present them enthusiastically to those around you.

Share Your Hot Buttons

When you share your hot buttons, be as specific as possible about your involvement. Employ plenty of facts, examples, dates, and places so your conversational partner has lots of free information to question you about. Your partner may not know much about the topic, but your enthusiasm will be contagious and will provide plenty of fuel for your partner to ask follow-up questions. Avoid talking about your own hot buttons too much; it's a common pitfall.

Take care not to use jargon or technical terms when discussing topics with people who aren't familiar with your hot button. Give them an inside look at what excites you about the topic, rather than overly specific details. Be sensitive to how much time you devote to your hot button without hearing again from the other person. It's all right to let someone know what turns you on, but be aware that the other person may not necessarily want to hear everything you have to say about that topic. If you get go-ahead signals (like several follow-up questions), then continue until you sense that the conversation should return to the other person.

Seek Common Interests

Many people are pleasantly surprised to find that people they meet share common interests. Through active conversation, you get closer to particular goals associated with that subject. Of course, the more interests you have and are able to discuss, the more fulfilling your conversations will be.

Remember that conversation is a means of experiencing many things that you have yet to experience directly, like traveling to far-off places or jumping out of airplanes. When

you share these experiences, both participants will profit
from the exchange. So keep Dale Carnegie's advice in mind:
find out the really big things in people's lives and encourage
them to talk about them. Seek someone else's hot button,
and be sure to reveal your own, too, and sustaining conversations will be easy.

Key No. 3: Balance the Two-Way Information Exchange

In a good conversation, the participants are aware of the
two-way information exchange passing between them.
This information exchange should be a balance between
talking and listening. Good conversation is like playing a
game of catch. First one person has the conversational ball
and talks, and then after a bit tosses the conversation to
the other person. This "toss" can be in the form of a question, a request for an opinion, or a comment from the person whose turn it is to talk. Once your partner picks up the
conversational ball, he can carry the topic further or change
topics. By tossing the conversational ball back and forth,
the participants can balance the input and output of information about one another.

Good Conversation Is a Balance of Talking and Listening

For a conversation to be stimulating and sustained, the
participants must be active talkers as well as active listeners. Be sure to do both in conversation. Make a point of
throwing the conversational ball to the other person after
you have presented your ideas in an abridged form. Some
people feel they have to give long-winded explanations of
their views. This is usually unnecessary, confusing, and

even boring to your partner. It's better to paint the big picture first, and if your partner wants to know more, you can always fill in with details. Keep your comments and questions focused on big ideas rather than extraneous details, and you'll keep to the point. This way you won't confuse or bore your listener.

Balance the Information Exchange

While people speak, they should be exchanging basic personal information, ideas, opinions, facts, and details at about the same rate. This doesn't mean a tit-for-tat exchange, but rather a general balance within the context of the conversation. When the exchange of information is balanced, you can get to know one another at the same rate— little bits at a time. If your conversation is active, a lot of information will pass between you, and in the end each participant will learn quite a bit about the other.

This is a natural way of getting to know people, and it will promote trust while encouraging both parties to disclose more personal information. "Good listeners" may feel that they don't need to disclose information about themselves, and that their disclosures are dull and boring. They might think: "Who cares where I'm from, or what I do, or where I went to school?! I'll bore the person to death!" It's important to be a good listener, but being an equal participant is also very necessary and important.

If the participant discloses too much and the other discloses too little, then the conversation is unbalanced. An unbalanced conversation will make both parties uncomfortable. One might think: "I did all the talking. She just sat there like a bump on a log!" In contrast, the other person will be thinking: "He never shut up! It was nonstop gab —I almost passed out!"

It's easy to understand why an unbalanced conversation results in a negative impression. If the information flow is balanced, including ritual information (small talk) and more personal self-disclosures, then the participants will feel they have gotten to know each other in a natural and nonthreatening way. The more balanced your exchanges are, the more quickly you'll really get to know the person and the more likely the relationship will flourish.

Key No. 4: Discuss Topics That Are Important to You

It's essential to let others know what you consider important and meaningful. The best way to reveal your values and attitudes to others is to discuss topics of concern and interest to you. These could be religion, politics, or current events, but whatever the topic, take the initiative and disclose some of your feelings and values.

When you talk about events that are important to you, the other person gets an idea of your personality, and it also provides an enormous well of conversational material.

What makes you tick? Why do you feel the way that you do about things? What are your concerns? What is your vision for the future? What are your likes and preferences? The answers to these questions tell others how you relate to the world around you.

Small talk is not just meaningless and shallow. You must realize that ritual questions and self-disclosure provide an environment for revealing more personal thoughts and feelings and also give more credibility and consistency to your views.

While expressing your ideas, you may hear yourself say things you have never said before. For many, conversation is when their ideas are formulated and developed into orderly concepts for the first time. When you discuss different ideas, it's important to do it in such a way that the other participant knows he is entitled to his opinion, too—even if it differs from yours. Be receptive to your partner's point of view and listen carefully to what he has to say. When it's your turn to give your opinion, your partner will be more receptive and open to your ideas.

A few words of caution: when telling someone what's important to you, be careful not to "spill your guts" or "tell all." Don't complain mercilessly about things you or your listeners can't do anything about. Leave very personal secrets out of your conversation, especially in the early stages. There is a time to tell friends things about yourself that are more personal. Wait until the time is right, and you've established trust. By disclosing what's important in a natural way you will let others in on what's important in your life.

Key No. 5: Change Topics Using Free Information

Changing topics is probably the easiest way to sustain a conversation while fishing for mutual interest areas with your partner. You don't have to talk out one topic before proceeding to the next. Good conversations are normally an interweaving of subjects and ideas, and it's not uncommon for participants to jump from point to point. It's helpful to stay within generally related subject areas, but if your discussion proceeds into new areas, you can always return to the original topic.

Dear Gabby,

I'm lunching with a client, and I don't want to talk about business since our morning and afternoon are concerned with business. How do I make interesting informal conversation during lunch?

Thank you,
Interested

When you are with a client, it is important to know something about her outside interests. In many cases you can obtain this information in advance, and usually, if you lis-

ten carefully, through free information. Doing your home-
work prior to a planned meeting can make a big difference
when it comes to casual conversation. Find out what your
client's personal interests are and you're on your way to
closing the deal. When you sit down to lunch, simply say, "I
understand you are quite a flower gardener. How long have
you been involved in that?" or "I read an article of yours in
Garden magazine. I enjoyed it very much. Do you mind if I
ask you a question about my garden?"

If you don't have any inside information about the person, be particularly attentive for free information. Perhaps
the person will mention in passing about being in Hawaii
for a business conference. You can say, "I heard you mention earlier that you were in Hawaii. Did you enjoy your stay
in the islands?" or "Had you been there before?" or "Which
island did you like the best?"

Be sure to reveal plenty of free information about yourself
throughout the conversation. When you sense a certain
topic has been talked out, then change the subject by refer-
ring to some free information revealed earlier, or offer some
new information of your own. Say: "It's interesting to hear
you talk about sailing, because I like it as well. In fact, I just
got back from a two-week trip off the coast of California,
and it was great!"

Refer to Free Information—
"I Heard You Mention Earlier . . ."

The most common method of changing topics is to refer to
previously revealed free information by commenting or asking a ritual question. You might say: "I remember you men-
tioned earlier that you were in Hawaii last month. Were you
there for business or pleasure?" Always listen carefully and
remember free information since it can provide good conversational fuel. If the topic you've been discussing has run
its course, just change the topic by inserting an open-ended
ritual question based on your own or your partner's free
information.

Sometimes you might want to change to another topic for only a brief moment. All you have to do is say: "Excuse me, but I'd like to change the subject for a moment," and then make your comment or ask your question. Try to complete your ideas quickly and then return to your original topic of discussion.

Be careful to maintain focus. Lack of focus gives your partner the impression that you cannot (or don't care to) discuss a particular topic on a meaningful level, and therefore are avoiding the topic. It may also indicate that you are not listening or that you are bored with the subject matter —both of which may be true! If your partner gives you a brief response, she may not wish to discuss the topic for a particular reason. Be sensitive to unenthusiastic responses, and be ready to change to a new topic quickly when you feel you have touched on a high-sensitivity or low-interest area for the other person.

Let's Change the Subject!

What do you do if someone brings up a negative or inappropriate subject—especially at a party or social event? These are subjects that are in poor taste, "downers," or generally unhappy topics which make people uncomfortable. For example, if someone makes a racial slur in an attempt to be funny, to attract attention, or to get a conversation going, you can show that you don't have the same opinion. Do so without a lot of emotional discussion. Simply say: "I don't really agree with that," or "I'm sure we can find more pleasant things to talk about," or "I'll forgive you for asking that question, if you'll forgive me for not answering it."

You've made the suggestion to change the subject, so it's up to you to do just that. Pick up the conversational ball quickly and open a new topic of discussion by making a comment or asking an open-ended question based on free information that you heard earlier before the conversation took an unfortunate turn. Usually the other participants will feel relieved that the negative topic didn't last too long.

Listen for Key Words, Facts, and Details —and Remember Them!

Listen carefully for key words, facts, and details, and refer to them as your conversation continues. This shows that you are listening, interested in what is being said, and it also serves as conversational fuel. You can control the conversation's direction simply by focusing your comments and questions on these facts and details.

Your conversations will progress along a pathway of exchange. Once you discover mutual interest areas, you can continually return to and explore them as new ideas come to mind.

Key No. 6: Seek Out Common Interests and Experiences

Suppose you meet a person and you really hit it off? Usually you'll think: "I really like this person. We have a lot in common. I can relate to his feelings and emotions. We have fun together. We get along well. I can be myself. He listens to me and understands what I'm talking about."

It's important to let your conversational partner know when you can identify with him. When you can relate to something directly or indirectly, respond in a way that lets your partner know you are listening and understanding and can personally identify with it. For example, if you are discussing someone's recent trip to a location where you have visited, lived or are preparing to visit, interject a quick comment or question based on your experience about that place, such as: "I used to live there," or "I was attending school there," or "What's it like there?" or "I'm due to go out there next month."

Quick inserts will provide your conversational partner with immediate feedback and let him know that you can relate to the subject. Make quick connections and you can direct the flow of the conversation in a natural way. When you couple this with open body language and active listening, you are signaling your partner to continue with the topic. In this way, you can identify areas of mutual interest and experiences as the conversation occurs. When there is a slight lull in the conversation, you can always refer back to an area of mutual interest. If you don't let the other person know that you relate to several details of his conversation, then you lose many areas of fruitful conversation.

When you make connections with your partner's experience, you also give him free information to pick up on. Remember, most people have many interests, and they want to find which interests you have in common. Let your partner know by saying: "Oh, really! I like that too!" or "Me too!" or "Gee, I don't meet many people who are interested in that, too."

When you let the other person know you can identify with a topic, experience, or goal, you create a bridge between you and him. Each bridge that you build gives you the opportunity to return for more conversation. The more bridges you build, the more you will be able to share with one another.

When you meet someone and discover areas of common interest and experience, you gain building blocks to develop a deeper relationship. Remember, much of the point of conversation is to discuss different topics and experiences in order to find a common bond. This gives you and your partner an opportunity to decide if you would like to get to know one another better. If you have enough in common, then hopefully you will want to see each other again to share common interests. So, when you discover a connection, tell your partner right away. This creates a sense of familiarity and indicates your interest in discussing the topic further and sharing your ideas. This is the stuff that friendships are made of.

4 Getting Your Ideas Across

SEVERAL FACTORS CAN KEEP THE SPEAKER FROM GETTING HIS ideas across to others. People have a *resistance to change* for many different reasons. We are creatures of habit, and we tend to hold on to certain ways of thinking, feeling, and behaving. Our fixed attitudes provide real or imaginary gains, and we feel comfortable and free from the fear of being taken advantage of. Resistance to change is reinforced by the attitude that it's safer *not* to trust people.

Another common problem which complicates reaching others is that sometimes you are competing for their attention. Instead of listening to your every word, the other participant is often *thinking* her own thoughts and tuning you out. Because of her low listening and attention span, your ideas and arguments become lost or misunderstood. Common signs of wandering attention include your partner asking unnecessary questions, making irrelevant comments, and bringing up arguments that have already been discussed and answered. These factors indicate that the other person is not tuned in to your thinking, and isn't ready to adopt or consider your ideas.

A third factor that interferes with communication with others is *wishful hearing.* What you say is often misunderstood by the listener because he interprets it to mean something he really wants to hear—not what you actually said or intended. Wishful hearing can take the form of jumping to conclusions based on a few isolated facts or actions, and it results in giving meaning that originates only in the listener's mind.

A fourth reason why you may not get your ideas through to others is that you make *unwarranted assumptions* about the other person. You may assume that others know and understand many things that you take for granted. Unwarranted assumptions are reinforced when your partner remains silent and mechanically nods his head, implying acceptance or understanding and encouraging you to continue thinking that he is right with you.

When it finally appears that the listener doesn't have a clue about what you have been saying, the situation can become rather awkward. You will feel that you have been talking to yourself, and the listener will feel like an idiot.

Finally, people who maintain a veil of *habitual secrecy* about what they think and feel tend to be resentful when you ask them what they do or any other common ritual question. These people experience your curiosity as a threat to their security, and as a result, they tend to act defensive and unfriendly.

All of us have secrets, even from those we know and trust a great deal. This is natural. The degree to which a person keeps her thoughts secret determines her receptivity to outside influences and persuasion. Getting your ideas through to people who won't tell you what their ideas are is difficult. Such people have a low receptivity level and aren't likely to accept your ideas.

Opening Channels

Encouraging Cooperation and Receptivity

There are ways to overcome difficulties in presenting your ideas to others. Begin to encourage cooperation and receptivity by *telling others the purpose of your conversation.* "The reason I'm calling is . . ." or "I'm new in the neighborhood. Do you happen to know a good restaurant nearby?" or "I've always wanted to be able to do that! Will you show me how?" or "I'm going to be traveling there soon. Do you know . . ." or "I'd like to talk to you about. . . ." These types of self-disclosures create a sense of trust in you and will allow your partner to feel more comfortable in responding. If you don't gain your partner's trust, most likely she won't share opinions or feelings with you.

When you ask a question, tell the person why you want to know. If you don't reveal the purpose of your questions, the other person might feel nervous, suspicious, or uncomfortable. She may think you don't believe her and are trying to find out if she is really telling the truth. Tell your motivation for asking the question, and your partner will be more inclined to answer without being overly cautious.

Another essential factor in gaining people's cooperation and receptivity is *developing respect for others.* Many of our attitudes and feelings are communicated without words, and how we listen to other people's ideas tells them how we think and feel about them. When you show that you care, a person will more likely confide in and trust you. When you ask for someone's opinions, you're actually giving a compliment because you are saying that you value that person's viewpoint.

Don't ignore people's feelings, and you'll be encouraging cooperation and receptivity for you to present your ideas.

A good way to increase your sensitivity while talking to others is to ask yourself questions like:

"How will what I'm saying make the other person feel?"
"How will he react to what I'm saying?"
"Will he feel complimented or put down by what I'm saying?"

By *taking the other person's viewpoint,* you will be projecting your own receptivity and, as a result, will lower her defenses and open the channels of communication. It also makes you more aware of implied or hidden meanings accompanying conversation.

Explore Irrelevant Comments

When you hear ideas that seem irrelevant, explore their purpose. Don't insist that all comments be relevant by ignoring or dismissing comments that seem extraneous or off the subject. *Accepting the other person's sense of relevancy* will broaden the conversation to include his purpose as well as yours. This encourages your partner to cooperate with you because you're showing that you see things from his point of view. As a result, he'll be open to your ideas. Cooperation and receptivity increase when you show your partner that you consider his ideas as important and valid as your own.

5 Closing Conversations Naturally

ALL CONVERSATIONS MUST COME TO AN END SOMETIME. Since there's a natural flow to most conversation, there is a "right time" to bring conversations to a successful close.

The Best Time to End a Conversation

Whether you are engaged in a brief or lengthy conversation, be aware of the dynamics involved in ending conversations in a positive manner. If you wait too long, you and your partner will feel the strain and become uncomfortable, anxious, or even bored. The easiest moment to end the conversation has already passed.

If you are anxious, especially during short periods of silence, you may end the conversation earlier than necessary, and in an abrupt manner. This will leave your partner with the impression that you don't feel positive about the conversation (or your partner).

It's best to end a conversation after both parties have expressed themselves to one another, and when the time seems right (or demands) for you to go your separate ways.

It's important to end conversations in a warm and engaging manner, so that you'll both feel good about the exchange that has occurred.

Closing Conversations in a Positive Way

There are natural pauses between sentences and topics of discussion, and it's wise to wait for these opportune moments to bring your conversations to a close.

When you feel the time is right to close the conversation —that is, the discussion has come to a conclusion, or one of the parties has to leave—take an active role and begin to send signals that you are ready to leave. Briefly summarize the main ideas your partner has been expressing. This shows the other person that you were listening and that you understood, and it also signals a conclusion to the discussion.

If you are discussing a particular current event, and you want to send a conclusion signal, you could say "It certainly sounds like you're well informed about the problem. I'll read that article you were talking about."

After you send a signal that you want to end a conversation, it's good to plan to see the other person again (only if you really want to) by setting a meeting for the future. Instead of closing with the customary cliché, "Why don't we get together sometime?" (which usually means never), be more specific about an event such as a movie or dinner, and a time within the next week or so.

In a friendly and direct way you could say: "I've really had a lot of fun talking with you, _____. How about getting together next week for dinner or a movie? I'll give you a call."

In this way, you express your interest in your partner while leaving an open invitation to meet again. This is particularly effective for developing friendships and relationships.

Remember to use your partner's name when you say good-bye, and use open, friendly body language (eye contact, smiling, and a warm handshake). Then be on your way. Avoid long, drawn-out good-byes.

Getting Out of Problem Conversations

There are times when the nature of a conversation, or the person you're speaking with, makes you prefer to end the conversation and withdraw without offending the other person. If you are cornered by a long-winded bore at a party who has been bragging about his exploits for some time, then try the following strategy to end the conversation.

Wait for a slight pause between words or sentences, and then quickly interject (an acceptable form of interruption) a few rapid yes or no questions, thus interrupting the bore's flow of words and giving you the conversational ball. (Remember, you can direct a conversation by asking questions.) Then restate in a few sentences (make an effort to be positive) an acknowledgment of your partner's last few statements, and make your getaway. You can say: "Well, it sounds like you enjoy your work! Good luck on your next project. I'm going to mosey along and say hello to a friend of mine," or "I'm going to get some hors d'oeuvres now, if you'll excuse me." After smiling and shaking hands, say: "Talk to you later, George," and then move directly out of the situation.

You may be worrying, "But what if I don't know anyone

else at the party! I can't just stand around! He'll see me standing there and become offended!" Try this simple solution: Go refill your glass, get a nibble to eat, or visit the bathroom, and then take a few moments to survey the situation. Look for the most open and receptive group or person in the room. Proceed there directly and engage in conversation. If you're really sharp, you can spot your likely person or group before you deliver your conversation closer.

Handling the Complainer

The complainer usually talks about personal problems, misfortune, sickness, and other unpleasantness. In most cases, people who focus on negative topics are looking for sympathy. No one enjoys listening to the constant complainer. Therefore, after listening for free information and details of the problem, ask a few yes/no or closed-ended questions to break the flow of complaints and to allow you to direct the conversation to a conclusion.

Express some words of sympathy such as, "It sounds like you're having a tough time," or "I'm sorry to hear that you're having so much trouble." This will indicate to the other person that you have been listening and empathize with her problem. You might cheer the person up with a bit of a jest like: "Is it really as bad as all that?" Smile and use strong eye contact to show you are trying to add a little humor to the situation.

When handling the complainer, it is perfectly acceptable to offer a few words of unsolicited advice or general words of wisdom and encouragement such as: "Just hang in there —it'll work out," or "If it makes you feel any better, you're not the only one who is having that problem." Then with a sincere feeling say: "I hope things work out for you," smile, give the person a warm handshake, and say: "I'm going to go say hello to a friend of mine." Then say good-bye, using the person's name, and move quickly out of the situation. Don't act guilty about departing by taking too much time to close the conversation.

Dealing Assertively with the Manipulator

We've all been in conversations where the person we are speaking with is attempting to make us do something against our wishes. It could be a high-pressured sales pitch or a pushy boss who wants you to work late for the fifth night in a row. In these cases, the goal is to end the conversation in a positive manner and not be forced to do something against your wishes.

For the persistent salesperson, say: "I appreciate your enthusiasm, but don't waste any more of your time. I'm not interested. Thank you anyway." When the salesperson doesn't take no for an answer, calmly restate your response, "I'm not interested," over and over again. This effective technique is referred to as the "broken record" and allows you to maintain persistence without arguments and thus avoid manipulation.

When you are ending a conversation with your boss who wants you to work late, it's important to end the conversation on a positive note, but show that you will do what *you* want to do—and still have a job when you arrive for work the next day. Start by stating assertively what you want, while you let your boss know that you understand and sympathize with the problem. The conversation might be as follows:

Boss: Diane, Jean won't be coming in, so I'm going to need you to stay late tomorrow to finish those reports.

Diane: Gee, Mr. Lund. That's impossible. I have something planned for right after work, and can't miss it.

Boss: Well, you'll just have to change your plans, or be late, because the main office wants those reports in by the next day, or it will be my neck.

Diane: I'd like to be able to help you, Mr. Lund, but I won't be able to work late tomorrow night.

Boss: You've always been so reliable before, and now

you're letting me down. This is really putting me in a tough spot!

Diane: I understand how you feel, but I won't be available. This is something I've been planning for a long time, and if I miss it, I'll be very unhappy.

Boss: But who am I going to get to finish up those reports?

Diane: I don't know, but I'm sure you'll be able to work something out.

Boss: I don't think Jean will be in on Tuesday either. I'd like you to work late Tuesday too.

Diane: Knowing Jean, you're probably right, but I won't be able to work late Tuesday either.

Boss: Diane, this is really disappointing. You've always helped me out in the past.

Diane: That's true, Mr. Lund, but I won't be available for overtime all this week. Have you thought about giving Jeff a call? He said he was looking for some extra work. Maybe he can help.

Boss: Jeff? That's an idea. He might be the solution.

Diane: Good. I'm sure Jeff would be happy to do the job.

Boss: Okay Diane, thanks—oh, and have a good time tonight.

Diane: Thank you, Mr. Lund.

This conversation requires restating your position in positive terms to the other person (maintaining persistence through the use of "broken record"), sympathizing with the problem, and possibly offering a potential solution or compromise. By not overreacting in a defensive or negative manner, Diane was able to do what she wanted while helping her boss solve his staff problem.

To summarize, when you end conversations:

- Always attempt to end the exchange on a positive, friendly note. This lets the other participant feel good.
- Use the other person's name, add a compliment such

as: "It's been great talking with you," and then say good-bye with a handshake or a kiss.

• Attempt to meet the person again for a specific activity at a time not too far into the future—say a week or so. Say: "I'm looking forward to seeing you again."

• Assertively tell your partner you enjoyed the conversation and you are going to mosey on to chat with someone else, get a drink, say hello to a friend, or whatever you wish to do, and then do it.

• Keep your good-bye short and sweet, and most of all warm and friendly.

Suggestions for Better Conversations

6 Remembering Names

HOW MANY TIMES HAVE YOU BEEN STANDING AND TALKING TO someone you've met before—maybe even more than once—and you can't remember her name? Or you're introducing mutual friends and acquaintances, and the names just slip right out of your mind? Or you go to a party and you're introduced to someone, and five seconds later you can't recall his name? Or maybe you see a client, and you can't remember her name to introduce her to your boss? These uncomfortable situations can make you avoid those you already know, as well as new people, for fear that you might offend them by forgetting their name.

Remembering Names Can Be Mastered

Most people recognize the enormous value in remembering names, but usually they say: "I'm terrible with names." With some technique and practice, recalling names can be mastered.

People Feel Special When You Remember Their Name

When you remember a person's name you've recently met, you make him feel important and special. You thus add a large measure of personal warmth and friendliness to the conversation, and create receptivity and openness with those you meet and see for a second or third time.

Why Do We Forget People's Names?

The primary reason why we forget people's names is *interference.* Interference is defined as any mental or physical activity that distracts our concentration during the introduction. A major mental distraction is our own mental inhibitions. We often think other things while being introduced, and as a result, we block out the name as it is being said. People think about personal details, and how they appear to the other person, as well as countless other thoughts.

Studies show that we forget what we learn very shortly after we have learned it. This is why most people forget the names of those they meet within five seconds of the introduction. Your mental state at the time of the introduction has a lot to do with how well you listen and absorb the person's name. When you are excited, distracted, anxious, full of self-doubt, or defensive, learning and retaining names proves to be difficult, if not almost impossible.

Breaking the Mental Block— Don't Think, Listen!

It is common not to hear a person's name at the moment of introduction when you face and speak to one another for the first time. Instead of listening carefully and registering the other person's name, most people are thinking about what they will say next. This inward focus creates anxiety

automatically and sets the trend for the ensuing conversation. Often this results in a short, unsustained exchange.
We forget the names of those we are introduced to because
in reality, we never learn the name in the first place.

Concentrate Your Complete Attention on the Introduction—Repeat the Name

Let the other person know that you consider his name important by giving him your full attention when you are introduced. Look at the person directly with eye contact, give
a friendly smile, and extend a warm handshake. When the
person says his name, say: "Nice to meet you, _____." Let
the person you are meeting know that you are interested
and want to learn his name.

If you didn't hear the name the first time, simply say:
"Excuse me, but I didn't hear you. What's your name
again?" Be sure to repeat it to make certain you're right. If,
after the person repeats his name a second time, you still
don't understand, then ask him to spell his name. This is
particularly effective in learning foreign or unusual names.
After you understand the name, repeat it to yourself several
times and use it frequently during the conversation.

Take a Mental Picture of the Moment of Introduction

Create a detailed mental image of your situation and the
immediate surroundings of the introduction, and you will
be provided with several additional clues to help you remember people's names. Allow a clear image of the person's
face to form in your mind while you visualize her name as
well. A person's forehead is a good place to visualize her
name. As the person speaks, observe her eyes and lips mov-
ing, and allow your image to fill in even more. A mental
picture can include any physical features, facial expres-
sions, mannerisms, posture, tone of voice, or even clothing
—any item or activity that makes her unique to you.

Associate the Name
and an Outstanding Feature

Mr. Firestone might have red hair or Ms. Greenwich may have beautiful green eyes. When direct associations between the person and his name are obvious, then use them. More often there are no real connections between a person's name and his appearance or occupation. In these instances, use your imagination and create associations from improbable details.

Observe unique or outstanding personal features and you can create associations that will help you to remember names. For example, suppose you are introduced to Ms. Robbins and you notice she happens to have a birdlike nose. If you associate *Birdlike nose* and *Robbins* at the introduction, when you meet again, that association should come to mind immediately and remind you of her name.

When someone is introduced to you, some associations should immediately take place. Usually you have enough time before speaking to select the person's outstanding feature, usually the one you notice first. Relax and give your complete attention to the person, and an association will quickly come to mind. This takes concentration and practice, but greater self-confidence will be the result. Be sure to employ the mental process of forming associations as you are introduced. In a short period of time, it will become almost automatic.

Look for Clues to a Person's Name

A clue is an item that you can easily associate with a person's name to remind you of all or part of his name. For example, if you meet Graham, and you notice a few streaks of gray hair near his temples, then this could serve as a clue. Make the association right away—and don't be inhibited by the form that the association takes. Very likely you will think "Graham" when you see those few gray hairs the next time you meet. Other clues to Graham's name might be his *gray* clothing, his *gra*ciousness, his *gra*ve mannerisms, or his *gra*cefulness.

If you can't recall a name instantly, go back mentally to the moment of the introduction and say the clue over and over again until it triggers the name. For Graham you would say: *"Gra . . . Gra . . . Graham!"* It's okay to guess if you think you might know, but you aren't certain. Use clues to trigger remembering a person's name.

Here is another example. The name is Marcey McClean. You observe that she is well-dressed. Associate her appearance as *clean* and connect it with *McClean*, and remembering her last name will be easy. If you associate *sea* with *clean*, you will have a hint for her first name as well. Thus, you will most likely be able to trigger recalling *Marcey McClean.*

Don't Let Mental Inhibitions Block First Associations

There will be many times when associations you make with a person's name may not be particularly flattering. Quite often they can be rude and insulting. Mental inhibitions can block first associations when they are not complimentary to the person. Telling yourself, "I shouldn't be thinking about this person in this way," you might try to think of something more positive. By that time, the moment for really making that name stick in your mind is past.

Remember, associations are to help *you* remember names, not to express how you might feel or think about the person. Let the first association that comes to mind, whether complimentary or insulting, connect with the person's name. You aren't going to tell her *how* you remembered her name, you're just going to say the name. The person will be flattered that you have remembered her name, and she won't care how you accomplished it.

An Alternative Method—Choose a Unique Feature and Isolate It

Look at a person carefully. When you've selected a unique feature, allow it to float away from the person and into some association with all or part of the name. For example, if it's Benny Fields, and the outstanding feature is a big nose, let the big nose float and land in a field. The association of a big nose in a field should trigger *B . . . Field, B . . . Field, Benny Fields.* In many cases, and with practice, you will need only one or two associations to recall the complete name. Remember, if the name doesn't come to you immediately, return to the moment of introduction and replay it several times in your mind.

You can isolate a person's outstanding feature and associate it with his name very quickly. Usually you will have enough time to observe someone and choose a unique feature before you are even introduced. When you acquire the habit of forming associations in this way, you have half the association ready for the name. Soon you will be making associations almost instantaneously, and your ability to recall names will quickly improve.

The Trick to Remembering a Long Chain of Names

Nearly everyone has been in a situation where there is barely enough time to shake hands with one person, and you are already being introduced to someone else. In many cases, there is less than a second or two between introductions. Surprisingly, you can form associations very quickly if you use your imagination, self-confidence, and experience gained through practice.

Focus on Common First Names

Think of all the people you have met with the name Robert, Diane, Steve, or Mary. When you meet a large group, many will have the same names as people you already know; perhaps even a good friend or family member.

Associate the "New Mary" with the "Old Mary"

When you meet someone with a common first name, think of someone with the same name, and associate. It's best to choose the *first* person you think of and ask yourself how much the "new Mary" looks or acts like the "old Mary." In what ways are they opposite? For instance, is the new Mary tall and the old Mary short? Imagine them side by side in your mind. Use your imagination and powers of observation and finding a common or opposite characteristic or feature will be easy. Focus your attention on the person while selecting a feature that will help you remember her name.

Repeat the Names Out Loud

When you are introduced to a group, repeat each name aloud. This will let the person know you care about knowing her name. It will also let you know immediately whether you have the correct name, and will reinforce the important moment of introduction so you can recall it later. After you have been introduced to everyone, attempt to repeat all the names in a row. If you have been making associations while you were introduced, you will probably get several right. Ask anyone whose name you can't remember to repeat it for you, and the person will almost always do so. Most people aren't offended if you didn't remember their name in this type of situation, and they will be surprised and impressed if you do.

Take the First Letter from Each Name and Make a Letter Chain

A letter chain is a real or made-up word or abbreviation based on the first letter of the names of people you have met in a group. Forming a letter chain from the first initials of each person's name can be helpful in remembering up to five or six names. Suppose you are seated around a table and you're introduced to Midge, Albert, Larry, Terry, and Oscar. The letter chain would be M-A-L-T-O. You might think that this method will work only if the letter chain spells out an actual word, but this is not necessarily so. Let's say the names are Mary, John, Bob (MJB), plus Phil, Hilary, and Diane (PHD). To remember the names (they don't have to be sitting in this order) just link the two sets of letters together: MJBPHD. Letters can be combined in *any* sequence that helps you give an order to the names and triggers recall.

During a free moment, repeat the letters and their corresponding names to yourself a few more times. The more you repeat the names, the stronger they will stick in your mind. If you think of a better association to fit with a name, then make it. Look for hidden clues that will help you remember the letter chain, such as the initials of your favorite brand of cereal, or the call letters of a local television or radio station.

Make Up a Story Chain of Last Names

Story chains are an effective technique for remembering last names. Suppose you are seated around a conference table and introductions begin with Ms. Hauser. Immediately picture yourself in a house. The next name is Brewster. Now picture yourself in the house drinking a beer. The next person introduces herself as McGillicuddy. Now imagine yourself in the house, drinking a beer, drunk to the gills. Mr. Hall is next, and now you see yourself in the house, drinking a beer, drunk to the gills, and staggering down the hall. And the story can go on and on.

After the introductions are complete, repeat the story chain in your mind, and review the names. To remember the fourth person's name, all you have to do is to go through the story and stop at the fourth person, and chances are you will recall his name.

Combining Several Techniques

Whether you are introduced to one person, a small group of four to six, or a large group of up to thirty, you can use a combination of several methods to remember names.

Here are some examples of several kinds of quick associations to help you remember names, especially in a medium-to-large group. A person is wearing gaudy jewelry and her name is Julie. For a bushy-bearded man named Bob, think of those *B*'s in Bushy-bearded Bob. Johnson's big ears remind you of the letter *J*. Flora is seated not far away from a floral arrangement. Richard has a beard like the one Richard Burton sometimes has. Jane's beautiful long black hair reminds you of an old friend with the same name. And the associations can go on and on.

Associations— With Practice— Can Form Instantly

You may think it takes a long time to form associations about the people you meet. The opposite is usually true, and with practice and confidence, associations become instantaneous. If you perform these mental operations habitually, your ability to learn and recall names, personal details and situations will improve tremendously.

Final Tips for Remembering Names

1. Establish direct eye contact and smile during the introduction.
2. Give your full attention to the introduction.
3. Listen carefully and repeat the name immediately.
4. Think of someone with the same name.
5. Form an association immediately with the name and her outstanding feature or anything else that will assist you to recall all or part of the name. The first association—complimentary or insulting—is best.
6. Don't worry if the association is not flattering.
7. Use the name frequently during the conversation.
8. If you have forgotten the name or didn't hear it the first time, ask the person to tell you again or even to spell her name.
9. Don't make excuses for yourself such as: "I'm terrible with names."
10. Interference and mental inhibitions are the main reasons for not remembering names.

7 Improving Your Conversations

Silence—It's Not What You Say, It's What You Don't Say

SILENCE HAS MANY MEANINGS. SOMETIMES PEOPLE FILL IN THE blanks with wishful thinking, and assume things are meant when they aren't actually said. Silence is neither a confirmation nor a denial, and it usually leaves a question or comment unresolved.

Silence—A Negotiating Tool

Silence can be used very effectively as a negotiating device. A salesperson can present a high-powered sales pitch,

speaking constantly and not giving you time to think about
what is being said. Silence gives you time to think about
what is being proposed. It can encourage you to come to the
side of the salesperson by providing "space" for you to talk
and think about your ideas.

Silence Is Okay

Silence is natural in a conversation. Words don't have to be
spoken all the time to communicate. Silence allows people
to experience their immediate environment without feeling
like they have to fill every void with a word. For some people,
a lack of talking can be uncomfortable and can cause great
anxiety. This is, for the most part, unnecessary. Silence
should be considered a time to rest or think about conversation topics. If, however, silence seems more a rule than
an exception, it can be a way of avoiding a particular topic
or issue which you really want to discuss but are afraid that
your partner will object to.

Use Encouragement and Positive Feedback— Don't Criticize

Even though there is always room for improvement, when
you are giving feedback it's better to praise the positive
attributes of someone's efforts first, even if you really have
to search for something good to comment about. It's also
important not to sandwich positive comments and con-
structive criticism together into the same sentence. Sand-
wiching praise and criticism together usually turns the
listener off and he becomes less cooperative and receptive
to your suggestions for improvement. It's better to give
praise where it is due and acknowledge the effort required
to complete the task. For example, to a child who has finally

finished an assignment which is way overdue: "I'm really happy to see that you've finished the assignment. It takes time to write a report that looks as good as this." Then to correct the problem of late work, you could say, "How do you think you might be able to get your next assignment in on time?" By encouraging the child with positive feedback and then presenting the problem in the form of an open-ended question, you make it more likely that the child will respond enthusiastically to the next assignment, as well as get the work done on time.

Playful Teasing Is a Healthy Way to Convey Feelings and Attitudes

Teasing, if it is carried out in a playful and upbeat way, can be beneficial and uplifting. Teasing sensitively, not maliciously, can be an important channel of expression from one person to another. When you convey what you think and feel in a lighthearted manner, people will be more likely to consider what you are saying.

Strategy for Dealing with Put-Downs

When you are criticized with a put-down, how should you react? Keep your sense of humor up and your defenses down, and you'll be in a better position to ward off cryptic comments and let the other person know you have a positive attitude about who you are and what you do.

Don't Lose Your Sense of Humor

B ring a bit of humor into a tense or boring situation by poking a bit of fun at the people involved—especially yourself. It is important for friends to be able to laugh at themselves and at each other. We never want to lose our sense of humor, because without it, our sensitivity to criticism becomes too high. Letting people tease you a bit and laughing at yourself can be helpful when times get tough and you begin to take yourself a little too seriously.

Put-Downs Can Be a Test of Your Self-Confidence

S ometimes people put other people down to see how they react under fire. If your reactions are defensive ones, chances are good that a sensitive spot has been hit. If you laugh at yourself, and don't take the put-down too seriously, then the other person will assume you are self-confident and secure.

Ask Open-Ended Questions to Find Out the Real Reason for Put-Downs

I nstead of reacting with "Why don't you lay off," or another defensive comment, try an open-ended question to encourage the other person to tell you what's really bothering him. This opens up the communication channels and hopefully ventilates some of the anger and frustration that causes people to put one another down. Following are some examples:

"Why do you feel that way?"

"What is it that seems to be bothering you?"

"I don't understand. What is it about ____ that is bad?"

"What is it that you don't like about ____?"

"What can I do to make you feel more positive about what I'm doing?"

The Other Person May Have Some Very Valid Things to Point Out to You

Once some of the real reasons for a person's anger come out, it's best to talk and seek a compromise solution to the problem. If a person's criticism of you is valid, try to omit responses with the words "but," "still," "however," and "yet," and substitute "You're right! What should I have done?"

The Best Way to Get What You Want Is to Ask for It Directly

Most people prefer to be asked directly to give or do something. Many people resent demands that are not out in the open. If you want something from someone, it's better to make your request clearly. In this way, the listener knows what you are asking for, and can answer yes or no to the request, and decide to what extent, if any, she is willing to cooperate. You can't always get what you want, but at least you'll have the satisfaction of knowing you made a direct effort.

People Can't Read Your Mind

Some people expect others to know what they think, feel, and want. These people send out hidden message after hidden message hoping that the other person will figure out what it is that they are asking for. It's better to be direct, because hidden messages are often ignored or misunderstood.

For example, consider the sulking lover who wants attention from his girl friend. He stands gazing into a field of people at the park while his girl friend chats with her friends nearby. He wants attention, but he doesn't want to ask for it directly, so he pouts and thinks: "I don't want to have to ask. She should know that I want her to come over here." As his girl friend looks over and sees him alone in what appears to be a pensive mood, she thinks: "If he wanted to talk, he'd signal me to come over or walk over. It looks like he wants to be alone for a while."

In this case, the boyfriend's hidden demands were not so much ignored as misinterpreted. He wanted attention, and she thought he wanted to be left alone. She can't read his mind, but that's what he expected her to do. Instead, she merely read his body language, and it seemed to say, "Stay away—I want to be left alone."

"What Do You Want From Me?"

When you recognize that a hidden demand is being made upon you, treat it like a direct demand—but make sure you understand clearly what the demand is. You can make a hidden demand direct by rewording what the person is saying and repeating it. "Do you mean to say that you want me to . . . ?" or "If I understand you correctly, you want me to . . . ?" These questions will clarify the demand, and then it's up to you to tell the person to what extent you are willing to carry out his request.

8 Overcoming Conversational Hang-ups

MANY CONVERSATIONAL PROBLEMS ARE THE RESULT OF misconceptions or negative attitudes toward those you wish to communicate with and/or yourself.

Most conversational hang-ups are rooted in fear. Frequently, they relate to how other people will judge you. These hang-ups tend to prevent you from reaching out to others in an honest and sincere way and they can be considered conversation blocks.

The most common conversational hang-ups and some ways of rationalizing them are:

1. *"I'm right—you're wrong!" (Arguing)*
   Always be right. Never lose an argument. Show others that your opinion is better.

2. *"I can read a person like a book."* (Stereotyping)
   Draw quick conclusions about those you meet based on isolated statements or actions.
3. *"It doesn't matter to me."* (Being non-assertive)
   Always go out of your way to please others, and they will like and respect you. Stay out of the decision-making process, to show that you are a flexible person. Don't do your own thing, because people may disapprove, or become offended or upset.
4. *"Tell me something I don't know."* (False modesty)
   Being a know-it-all will impress the people you talk with.
5. *"I'm boring."* (Copping out)
   Don't talk, because you don't have anything really interesting to say.

Hang-up No. 1—"I'm Right —You're Wrong!"

Some people think that good conversation means winning an argument or discussion. They present their *opinions* as indisputable facts. This type of conversationalist will go out of his way to show that his opinions are better than those of the people he's talking with. His goal is to never lose an argument, show that he is right, and *win* the conversation.

It's not uncommon for competitive conversationalists to put down other people's opinions by making comments like "That's the most ridiculous thing I've ever heard!" or "I think what you are saying is utter nonsense!" This attitude sends a clear message to the person you're talking with: "Since we differ in opinion, and I'm right—you are therefore wrong." There's another message that accompanies this communication: "Since I'm right, I'm better and smarter than you."

Needless to say, this closed and self-righteous attitude will not allow others to open up to you in any real, meaningful way—especially in the more emotionally sensitive areas. Manipulative put-downs make people feel foolish and stupid and as a result, tend to lower their level of self-esteem. This doesn't make them feel comfortable with you or allow them to feel as though they can trust you with more self-disclosures.

The misconception here is that people who feel they always have to be right or have to win a discussion think that others will respect their opinions more if they are rigidly committed to their view. As a result of this nonreceptive position, they send this signal to those they talk with: "Anyone who disagrees with me is obviously wrong, and therefore a fool!"

It's easy to see why *"I'm right—you're wrong"* can ruin a conversation and throw cold water on a developing friendship or relationship.

Don't Assume That Everything You Know or Believe Is Absolutely True

When discussing topics from differing points of view, remember there's a major difference between absolute fact and what we *assume* to be true. Often, our opinions are the result of preferences, biases, assumptions, and our conditioning—not necessarily facts. As a result, there are many gray areas where differences of opinions can be discussed (not argued) at great length with others. These areas are very fertile ground for good conversation.

Every person has the right to his point of view—even if it seems strange or totally absurd.to you—without being put down or ridiculed. Don't force your views upon others. Show a desire to understand your partner's point of view. Thus, you will encourage him to open up to you more and be more receptive to your ideas. This is especially important when you are trying to get your ideas and feelings across to others.

How to Say "I Don't Agree with You"

When someone says something you disagree with, avoid conversation killers like "You're dead wrong!" or "Where in heaven's name did you ever pick up such a stupid idea?" When you voice a difference of opinion, preface your statement with "It seems to me . . ." "Here's the way I see it . . ." "I think . . ." "I believe . . ." "It's my impression . . ." "In my opinion . . ." "I feel differently about it . . ." or "It's been my experience. . . ." When you present opinions this way, without condemning the other person's statement, she will be more likely to listen to what you are about to say, rather than putting up a defensive barrier to your ideas.

If someone disagrees with what you have said or believe, don't say, "You tasteless slob! Don't you know who you're talking to?" It's better to say "I guess we just regard this differently," or "I can see that you disagree. You're entitled to your own opinion," or "Well, different strokes for different folks!" If you don't like something and want to communicate this without offending the other person, say: "Well that may be a great piece of music (art, movie, play, etc.) but I didn't particularly care for it." Remember, you're entitled to your opinion, and so are the people you talk with. Be sure to send this signal clearly and the "I'm right—you're wrong" hang-up won't ruin your conversations.

Hang-up No. 2—"I Can Read a Person Like a Book!"

People who make this statement often form hasty conclusions from a person's individual comments or actions. When you jump to conclusions about someone, you may be unconsciously reacting to the person's stereotype. If your partner fulfills one characteristic of his stereotype, then that's all it takes to elicit this negative approach of "sizing him up."

People who judge others quickly are usually very critical of themselves and as overcritical of others. This negative attitude towards others serves to put them in a superior position while they put others down.

Some people have a tendency to express anger and self-criticism through criticism of others. They equate a single negative action or personality trait with a person's total behavior. Thus, if they see someone acting selfish, snobbish, or unfriendly in a particular situation, they assume she behaves this way all the time.

A critical attitude toward people's failings is a hidden way to put yourself down while putting other people down. It is an unfortunate approach to interacting with others and to solving your personal problems. It is a main reason why people jump to conclusions about others, and why these conclusions are usually negative.

Can You Tell a Book by Its Cover?

People who jump to conclusions about others based on single experiences are just as likely to believe that you can tell a great deal about a person by the automobile he drives, his occupation, and his clothing. Of course, you can learn about others from these details, but if you rely heavily on these, your conclusions are more likely based on previous experiences or preconceived notions. As a result, this method of learning about people evokes stereotypical images—not individual qualities. People don't like being stereotyped, and they sense when it occurs. Most likely they then will stereotype you also, and the communication channel closes.

Separate Specific Isolated Behavior From Total Personality

Reserve judgment about people until you have enough data to form a more accurate conclusion about what they are really like. Give the people an opportunity to get to know you in a real and meaningful way. Extend an open attitude towards others, and most likely the same attitude will be returned. If you are the victim of a put-down or a stereotypical remark that is not an accurate reflection of you, such as—"Boy are you ever a scatterbrained person!"—be sure to clarify that while you may sometimes seem a little scatterbrained, you are usually a pretty down-to-earth person.

Hang-up No. 3—"It Doesn't Matter to Me"

Some people believe that if they place other people's needs before their own, they will be liked and respected, and in addition, that people will return the favor sometime. People are often disappointed when this unrealistic expectation is unfulfilled. Some think that they are being taken advantage of and they become resentful.

People who say "It doesn't matter to me" are doing two different things. First, they are attempting to please others by seeking approval for their behavior. If they do what the other person wants, then what is there to disapprove of? Second, they are copping out and not taking the responsibility of being involved in the decision-making process that accompanies most activities.

It's Good to Be Flexible—but Not Indifferent

You might think that if you are amiable enough to do almost anything someone else wants (even if you'd rather not), this will make you an easy-to-get-along-with person. However, the other person might feel that your "It doesn't matter to me" attitude displays noninvolvement, indifference, or even boredom or insincerity.

Express Your Preferences (Even If They Might Be Contrary to Your Partner's)

If you don't express preferences, tastes, wants, and desires, people won't know what you like or what you are seeking. Most people are not mind readers, and unless you tell or show them what you want, they just won't know. If you don't express your true feelings, hostility, resentment, and guilt may result.

Assertiveness Pays Off

Assertiveness can be defined as "to state positively with confidence but with no objective proof." You have the right to do what you want and not to do what you don't want to do. You're entitled to feel the way you want about things, and you don't have to offer reasons or excuses for your feelings or behavior. (This is not to say that you are not responsible for your actions!)

Get What You Want by Asking for It

It's better to express what you want by asking for it instead of waiting for someone to guess what you want. Let someone know what you want, and he'll be in a better position to give it to you—or say no. At least you'll have the satisfaction of expressing yourself in an honest and direct manner even if you don't get what you want.

You Have the Right to Say No and Not Feel Guilty About It

If you don't want something, simply say no. People who have trouble saying no are usually afraid of offending or hurting the other person. If you say yes when you really want to say no, or you're not sure, say: "Let me think about it," or "I'll let you know," or "Let me call you back."

Offer an Alternative—Become Involved

If you say "It doesn't matter to me," you're not involving yourself in the decision-making process that accompanies human interactions. Instead of agreeing to all suggestions that come your way (even if you don't want to), offer some alternatives. Present your ideas and preferences, and your partner will gain a better sense of who you are, what you want, and your interest in the subject or activity. Become involved in the decision-making process. Don't passively accept anything, and others will know that you care. Involvement translates into interest, enthusiasm, and a desire to be with the other person.

"But What Will People Think of Me?"

Some people feel guilty about doing their own thing and feel that others may disapprove. They believe that people will find them selfish or that they will become offended or hurt.

If you do something that someone doesn't like, being afraid that she'll dislike you prevents you from pursuing your goals and needs. If you are manipulated in this way, you're overly sensitive to others' approval and what they think of you. You may be highly sensitive to rejection and fear losing your partner's love or support.

People Usually Upset Themselves

It's important to be sensitive to others' feelings. In most cases you don't hurt someone's feelings by doing what you want to do. The problem is how he interprets your actions. There are many different ways to react to the same event, and what's important is how *you* feel about what you're doing. If you act in your own interests, your self-esteem will be much higher than if you forgo your wants, needs, and goals because someone doesn't approve. Don't respond to the world around you based on "What will people think of me?" It's a frustrating and unfulfilling existence.

Do Your Own Thing

Stand up for your rights and do what you want. Do this assertively by telling others in direct and honest statements what your goals, intentions, and motivations are—*without feeling the need for their approval.*

When you think about what's important for you, try to look ahead a month or two—even further if possible—and project where you'll be as a result of your actions. Conceptualizing the future is often a key factor in making your pursuits realities instead of just unfulfilled dreams. Be assertive and you can acquire the satisfaction of knowing that you are giving your goals a good try, even if you don't succeed right away.

Caution: Assertiveness Is Not a Justification for Selfishness and Insensitivity

You may think that doing your own thing is an excuse or justification for being insensitive or uncaring about others. Friendships and relationships revolve around giving and receiving. Both are required, and a fair and equitable balance between the two is essential. Assertiveness allows you to take your needs into consideration, but don't discount the effect you have on those around you.

If being assertive and honest results in negative feelings and a loss of love, then maybe it wasn't love anyway. We can be manipulated in many ways—especially through threatening the withdrawal of love. This threat is a clear indication that manipulation is occurring.

Hang-up No. 4—"Tell Me Something I Don't Know"

Some people feel the need to project the image that they know everything and are good at everything. They are afraid they'll be considered incompetent and stupid if they don't pretend to know everything.

Being a "know-it-all" can effectively kill conversations because you convey the message that the other person's ideas and feelings don't matter to you. This cuts off the two-way exchange of information, ideas and feelings, and only serves to elevate you to a superior position at the other's expense. Considering the fact that we all have major limitations in our expertise and experience, this is a rather unrealistic and doubtful image to project to others. It becomes increasingly clear that you're just trying to boost your ego without honestly communicating.

It's Okay to Say "I Don't Know"

Saying "I don't know" is likely to make your partner respect you for your honesty rather than put you down for your ignorance. It's immature and overcritical to think that you (or anybody else) are required to know answers to every question or be aware of everything and everybody.

Suppose someone mentions a book, movie, or famous person in a discussion, and you nod your head knowingly as though you know exactly what he's talking about. It may come out later (as many times it does) that you didn't really have the direct experience you projected, and your partner will get the impression that you were just faking the conversation. This inhibits the conversation and your partner will tend to distrust your future statements and generally form a negative impression.

"I'm Not Familiar with That . . . Fill Me In!"

To overcome projecting a false image, admit your shortcomings, lack of experience, or ignorance about a certain subject, and look for your partner's response. In most cases (unless the other person is trying to put you down) your partner will accept what you know and don't know. It presents a balanced picture of you and tends to create a more trustworthy personal image.

Hang-up No. 5— "I'm Boring"

Some people take the easy way out and don't participate in conversations. They think that they have nothing interesting to say. This is a cop-out and self-imposed put-down. Copping out is an *avoidance technique* for not facing people, situations, and problems. Those who adopt this attitude are afraid of boring others or they don't want to make the effort required to carry on a conversation.

Don't Put Yourself Down

Don't be overcritical of yourself. If you think, "I don't know anything; I don't do anything; I live in a vacuum—I don't have anything interesting to say," this negative attitude suggests low self-esteem. Of course, others will quickly sense this attitude, and they will have the same idea about you.

Focus on the Positive Events in Your Life—And Talk about Them

Focus on the positive events in your life—events or experiences that you're excited about—and your enthusiasm will project to others. It's beneficial to talk about things that are important to you, and to express your ideas, opinions, and feelings. It tells others who you are and what's important to you, and it helps you understand yourself better. Don't cop out, and you won't be boring.

Don't Cop Out

Be aware of these common cop-out statements:

"I don't feel like it." (An excuse for not doing what you want or have to do.)

"I didn't have time." (Another excuse for not doing what you want or have to do.)

"What difference does it make?" (A rationalization for not putting out the effort required to make something happen.)

"I hate it when people ask me what I've been up to." (An avoidance response to someone showing interest in you.)

These hang-ups and cop-outs block the way to meaningful conversations, and they don't allow people to develop friendships and relationships. Usually, these attitudes are a matter of habit rather than deep psychological problems, and they can be overcome by changing your thinking and your approach to the people you interact with. Once you break the pattern of these hang-ups, you'll find a difference in how people relate to you. Others will notice a positive change in how you feel about yourself and about them. Your communication channels will be open and accessible to others and this will promote better conversations.

9 Making Friends

The Gift of Friendship

Making friends is a goal most of us have because we value companionship. Most people have only a few friends whom they trust completely with their most personal feelings and information. When you give someone your friendship, it becomes an important aspect of a relationship. Unfortunately, there are many who feel they have no one to confide in and call a good friend. This can change because good friendships can begin at any stage in your life.

What Is Friendship?

It has been said that love is blind, and friendship is just not noticing. Friends can be allies, supporters, or sympathizers who give encouragement, feedback, honest opinions, and usually a lot of advice. We reveal things to friends that we just wouldn't say to anyone else. A friend is someone you can trust with sensitive information and know that he won't hold it against you; someone who shares common interests and experiences with you and adds to your sense of fulfillment. Other components of good friendship are:

Patience	Stimulation	Sympathy	Intimacy
Respect	Equality	Fun	Spontaneity
Understanding	Reliability	Flexibility	Another Point
Sharing	Helping	Enrichment	of View
Compassion	Learning	Freedom	Tolerance
Trust	Love	Reassurance	Honesty

Making Friends Is Not Always Easy

Making friends takes time, effort, commitment, give-and-take, and a lot of tolerance for the many human frailties we all have. Although most people are open to new friendships, life pursuits such as careers and family tend to become a higher priority. Some people feel it takes too much time and effort to develop friendships.

Developing Trust

Another reason why friendships take time to develop is that they require mutual trust between people, and trust takes time to develop. To gain someone's trust, you must reveal some personal information and feelings so that the other person can gain a real sense of what kind of person you are, and what you are sensitive to. As time goes on, you and your friend will disclose more and more personal information, and the trust between you will grow. In the early stages of friendship, people sometimes don't know how much to reveal about themselves. If you are aware of the balance of information being traded back and forth, then your rate of self-disclosure will probably be appropriate.

A firm belief in someone's honesty and reliability can take quite a while to develop, while a breach of trust can destroy a relationship in a very brief period of time. When someone displays trust in you and confides in you, don't disappoint her by violating her faith and confidence in you.

To Meet People, Go Where You Have Fun

There are countless places to meet people, and there is little doubt that some places are better than others, especially to make contact with someone special. The "right place" could be a social event, church, political gathering, or even an adult education class. If you have a mutual interest, you're in the right place. When you meet someone in a place where you both enjoy the activities, you already have something in common and can begin developing a friendship.

Meet People Who Have Similar Interests

Suppose you are a beginning photographer, and you like to take rides into the country to shoot pictures. You have just gotten a new camera, and now you have decided to sign up for a beginning photography class. At the photography class, you will meet other people with at least one thing in common—photography. Many of your early conversations will probably focus around this topic and other related fields. Start your conversations by finding out the different reasons others are taking the class. You can ask questions like: "What do you hope to gain from this class?" or "How long have you been taking photographs?" or "How did you become interested in photography?"

How Friendships Begin

Think of all the people you meet and see at work, in your neighborhood, and especially at recreational or social events you attend. Many are potential friends and you can develop relationships with them.

Become Familiar with People

When you see the same people over a period of time, you can start conversations. Find out if you have something in common, and if the conditions are right, start up a friendship. Becoming familiar with the people you see often will make this much easier. Start by smiling and saying hello, and if the opportunity arises, introduce yourself.

Keep It Friendly—Nothing Too Heavy or Too Serious

After you have said hello a few times, you will most likely find an opportunity to stop and chat for a few moments. Maybe it's at work, walking down the street, or in the local food store. Show the other person that you are interested in getting to know him better by engaging in casual conversation. You don't have to be profound or too impressive. It's better to be informal, friendly, and receptive. *Remember:* Small talk sends the signal: "I'm interested in you, and open to conversation. Let's talk!"

Use Ritual Questions to Send the Message: "I Want to Get to Know You Better"

"How long have you been working here?"
"Have you lived in this neighborhood for a long time?"
"Where did you live before?"
"How did you get involved in this kind of work?"
"What do you like to do around here for entertainment?"

These ritual questions signal your interest, and give the other person the opportunity to express interest in you. As the person speaks, listen for free information, and pick up on these topics.

Finding Someone's "Hot Button"

The sooner you find out what turns someone on, the sooner you'll be able to establish whether you have anything in common. Sometimes you will know about a person before you actually meet. Look for objects that the person carries, such as a tennis racket, roller skates, artist's portfolio, or anything that might give you a clue to the person. Then ask, "I saw you walking the other day with a portfolio. Are you an artist?"

Keep an Inventory of Facts and Details About the Person

When you talk to someone and recall information he gave you in a previous conversation, he will be surprised and flattered. Comments like, "How's the job hunting going?" or "Have you had any luck at the track lately?" will show the other person that you were actually listening and that you care about what's happening in his life. This makes the person feel good—and important.

Be sure to concentrate fully on details that someone discloses to you, and make a point to remember key words and free information he provides. You'll be able to draw on this reservoir of information to sustain and direct later conversations.

Making the Other Person Feel Important

When you remember names and details of people you meet, you will make them feel special. Your attention demonstrates your interest and curiosity, and encourages them to talk and reveal more information. When people begin to open up, it shows they are gaining trust in you and are comfortable with you.

The Perfect Time to Introduce Yourself

When there is a pause in conversation, take the opportunity to say, "By the way, my name is _____. What's yours?" The sooner you introduce yourself, the easier it is. Generally, the longer you wait to make an introduction, the more uncomfortable it can get.

Show the Other Person You Like Her

When you want to make friends with someone, let her know you like her and want to get to know her better. Make it a point to stop and chat when the opportunity presents itself. You will be reinforcing a friendly, positive attitude. When you show a person that you like her, she will usually respond in a friendly manner.

Caution: Take care not to come on too strong to someone you have recently met. Be casual, informal, and comfortable. Take it slow and easy, and don't get too intense.

"How About Meeting Sometime for a Drink or a Cup of Coffee?"

During casual conversation with someone you want to become better acquainted with, suggest going out for some casual conversation over a drink, coffee, ice cream, or any other informal activity. This shows you like the person and want to spend time with him. If the person is available (there may be a boyfriend or girlfriend to answer to) and receptive, chances are they will say "Sure, why not!" Make an attempt to set a particular day and time by saying, "What's a good day and time for you?" or "How's tonight?" or "When's good for you?"

Dear Gabby,

I'm at work talking to a friend. I want to have dinner with him, but I'm afraid to ask. What should I do?

Hungry

Getting someone to share a meal with you isn't really so difficult when you figure nearly everybody eats at least one meal daily. When you are speaking to someone you already know slightly, at work or in any other situation, keep your ears open for a "food" hot button. It's easy to introduce the subject into conversation by merely asking questions about nearby restaurants, particular favorite foods, or memorable meals. Say: "Do you know any good restaurants around here?" or "How is the food at the restaurant on the corner?" or "Have you ever been to Louie's? I hear the food is excellent!"

Once you establish that you have some similar tastes in food, then suggest, "How about meeting for dinner one night next week? I know a great little place with great food and a fantastic atmosphere."

Usually if someone wants to spend time with you he will accept your open invitation. Now it's up to you to focus on a specific day and time. "What are you doing for dinner tonight? Are you interested in ＿＿ food?" is an easy way to ask someone to share a meal with you. If you expect to be taken out for dinner, then you will have to wait for an invitation. If you go dutch treat, there are no expectations attached, and either party can initiate the date.

Plan an Activity Around a Mutual Interest

After you spend some time together informally, suggest an activity you know the other person likes to do, and one that you are interested in, too. It could be going to a movie, bike riding, or going out to dinner. It won't matter as long as the event is mutually interesting, and the focus is on fun. You could make your proposal like this:

"Are you free for dinner tonight?"
"Would you like to see a movie tonight?"
"I know where there's a great band playing. Would you like to go dancing?"
"I'm in the mood for a walk on the beach. Would you like to join me?"
"Today is my exercise day. Do you want to play a few sets of tennis?"

"Hi, Karen, This Is Don. Do You Have a Few Minutes?"

Give your friend a call to confirm the time of your planned meeting, and just to say hello. Here are some tips for more comfortable telephone conversations.

- Get comfortable—preferably seated.
- When the person answers the phone, say, "Hi _____, this is _____. Have you got a few minutes to talk?" Always identify yourself and *never play* "Guess who this is."
- Ask a detail about how some aspect of the person's life is going, like "How's the writing coming along?" or "How did you make out with the job interview?"
- Tell the other person why you are calling. "I just wanted to confirm our meeting" or "I just thought I'd call to say hi."
- End your telephone call with a friendly comment like, "It's been nice talking with you," or "We'll be talking again soon," or "I'm looking forward to seeing you soon!"

Maintain Contact with People You Like

Once you've made contact with someone you like and find activities that you enjoy doing together, then continue to maintain contact so the friendship can grow. As time goes on, you and your friend can contact each other anytime you want companionship, assistance, or advice.

When you are asked to join an activity by someone, make an all-out effort to accept the invitation. This reinforces the other person's feelings of friendship towards you, and encourages her to share her experiences and activities. When you hear yourself say, "I really don't feel like it," this translates as disinterest. This doesn't mean you should do things you don't want to do, but be aware of the cop-out nature of this statement.

Be Open to New Experiences and Turn-ons from Others

Let your friends turn you on to new places, people, food, or anything else they want to share. This projects openness and receptivity to your friends' ideas, and allows them to feel good for turning you on to something they enjoy. This attitude creates a positive feeling toward you and your friends will become more receptive to the ideas and activities you suggest.

Share Activities with Your Friends

Take the initiative and ask your friends to share in activities that you enjoy. Make an effort to turn others on to some of the special places and events that interest you. This provides an opportunity for you to show others you like them, and reveals more information about you in subtle and indirect ways. Initiating an activity gives you greater control over the direction of the event and the surrounding conversation.

Friendships Grow and Develop in Time

Sometimes, friendships are like plants—they can grow slowly and steadily in time. Your friendship will grow as you share more experiences together. Time and shared experiences are important elements in friendships and can be expressed in these ways:

"We've been friends for a long time."
"We've gone through some pretty amazing times together."
"I don't know what I would have done without you."
"I want to thank you for all the help and support you've given me during the last couple of months. It's really made a big difference, and I appreciate it a lot."
"These last few months that we have spent together have been really fun. I've enjoyed them a lot!"

Dear Gabby,

I'm with an old friend whom I haven't seen for a long time. Where does the conversation begin?

Long-Lost Friend

When talking with old friends, it's important to re-establish old ties and bring each other up to date. Since there are many changes in our lives that happen over time, focus on the big events in your life. Talk about situations where you will be making decisions in the near future, and bounce your ideas off on your friend for feedback. This will help your decision-making process, and will also deepen your relationship.

It is equally important to seek out similar information from your friend. Chances are things have developed for him as well, and you may have to encourage him to talk about it. Find out how he feels about what he is doing, where he is going, or who he is involved with.

Sometimes old relationships need a little "priming" to get the words flowing again. However, once you get over those early feelings of "What can I say to this person that he doesn't already know about me?" the conversation will usually flow naturally.

"The Only Way to Have a Friend Is to Be One" —Ralph Waldo Emerson

It has been said that a friend knows all about you, but likes you anyway. For people to remain friends and friendships to grow requires flexibility and tolerance. Accept your friends as unique individuals with all the problems, hangups, and inconsistencies that all humans possess. If you accept your friends on these conditions, you will be much more likely to keep them. Do what you can for your friends, and when you are asked for a favor, then do it if you possibly can. It all comes back to you in friendship. If you are a good friend, you'll have good friends.

Friends Grow Together

When people find common interests they can develop individually as well as together, sharing these interests can enrich their lives and experiences. Developing and learning together is one of the most gratifying aspects of a relationship. In the best friendships, developing and learning never stops.

50 Ways to Improve Your Conversations

HERE ARE SOME FINAL REVIEW POINTS TO KEEP IN MIND WHEN HAVing conversations.

1. Be the first to say hello.
2. Introduce yourself to others.
3. Take risks. Don't anticipate rejection.
4. Display your sense of humor.
5. Be receptive to new ideas.
6. Make an extra effort to remember people's names.
7. Ask a person's name if you have forgotten it.
8. Show curiosity and interest in others.
9. Tell other people about the important events in your life.
10. Tell others about yourself, and what your likes are.
11. Show others that you are a good listener by restat-

ing their comments in another manner.

12. Communicate enthusiasm and excitement about things and life in general to those you meet.
13. Go out of your way to meet new people.
14. Accept a person's right to be an individual.
15. Let the natural you come out when talking to others.
16. Be able to tell others what you do in a few short sentences.
17. Reintroduce yourself to someone who has forgotten your name.
18. Be able to tell others something interesting or challenging about what you do.
19. Be aware of open and closed body language.
20. Use eye contact and smiling as your first contact with people.
21. Greet people you see regularly.
22. Seek common interests, goals, and experiences in the people you meet.
23. Make an effort to help people if you can.
24. Let others play the expert.
25. Be open to answering common ritual questions.
26. Get enthusiastic about other people's interests.
27. Balance the giving and receiving of information.
28. Be able to speak about a variety of topics and subjects.
29. Keep abreast of current events and the issues that affect all of our lives.
30. Be open to other people's opinions and feelings.
31. Express your feelings, opinions, and emotions to others.
32. Use "I" and speak of your feelings when you talk about personal things.
33. Don't use the word "you" when you mean "I."
34. Show others that you are enjoying your conversations with them.
35. Invite people to join you for dinner, social events, or other activities for companionship.

36. Keep in touch with friends and acquaintances.
37. Ask other people their opinions.
38. Look for the positive in those you meet.
39. Start and end your conversation with a person's name and a handshake or warm greeting.
40. Take time to be cordial with your neighbors and co-workers.
41. Let others know that you want to get to know them better.
42. Ask others about things they have told you in previous conversations.
43. Listen carefully for free information.
44. Be tolerant of other people's beliefs if they differ from yours.
45. Change the topic of conversation when it has run its course.
46. Always search for another person's "hot button."
47. Compliment others about what they are wearing, doing, or saying.
48. Encourage others to talk with you by sending out receptivity signals.
49. Make an effort to see and talk to people you enjoy and have fun with.
50. When you tell a story, present the main point *first*, and then add the supporting details afterward.

Here are all the tips and communication skills you need to begin and sustain conversations. Now it's up to you to get out there and meet people. You'll find that with practice, patience, and a positive attitude, you have nothing to lose and a lot to gain. Taking part in stimulating and rewarding conversations will become a reality. All you have to do is look somebody in the eye, smile, and start a conversation!

... of "How to Start a Conversation" can ... for $7.95 (plus $1.00 for shipping and handling charges) by sending a check or money order to:

"How to Start a Conversation"
NETWORK FOR LEARNING
P.O. Box 211
70 Greenwich Avenue
New York, N.Y. 10011